CHAPTER ONE

Thirty minutes before the brick smashed through his living room window Detective Inspector Liam O'Reilly was engaged in a one-sided argument with a rather obstreperous cat. Half an hour before he read the note attached to the brick and realised his life was about to change forever the Irish detective was fighting a losing battle with the ginger tom.

"It's a cat flap. You're a cat – so use it."

He gave the newly-fitted flap in the bottom of the back door a nudge with his foot to demonstrate what he meant.

Bram, the overweight tom wasn't budging. He looked up at O'Reilly, miaowed a couple of times and ambled off in the direction of the living room.

"Bloody cat," O'Reilly said and switched on the kettle to make some tea.

"Are you fighting with Bram again?"

O'Reilly turned around to see his daughter standing in the doorway. Assumpta had moved to Guernsey to live with her father earlier in the year. She'd been reluctant at first – the slow island life had taken quite a bit of getting used to but she'd soon got into the swing of things.

"Why bother to have a cat flap?" O'Reilly said. "If the dumb moggy doesn't even know how to use it?"

"He'll get used to it."

"That mangy beast is an idiot."

"Bram is not an idiot."

"Do you want some tea?" O'Reilly asked to change the subject.

"Thanks. I'm not going in to work for another couple of hours. I've got a follow-up to do on that Durand-Simon feud thing, but I can do that here at home. The weather out there is dreadful."

"How many follow-ups are you going to get out of those families?"

"As many as the people of the island want to read. That story was big news and the more I dug into the history of the two families the more dirt rose to the surface."

"Well, I'd prefer to put the whole thing behind me," O'Reilly said. "That was one of the worst investigations I've ever been involved in. And shouldn't you tread a bit carefully now? What with old Durand's suicide?"

"I'm a journalist, Dad," Assumpta reminded him. "It's what I do and at least the Gazette will approach the whole thing with a bit of integrity. The Herald couldn't give a hoot who they upset. What about you? Anything juicy on the go at the moment?"

"If a string of thefts from some containers down at the docks can be considered juicy, then yes."

"Sounds intriguing."

O'Reilly handed her the tea. "It's not. It's about as juicy as a shrivelled-up peach, but at least it's better than a murder investigation. I'd rather give one of those a miss for a while."

O'Reilly had only been on the island for six months and in that time, he'd faced more dead bodies than he had in his entire career in the Special Detective Unit affiliated to the Gardai in Dublin. He'd made the move to the island in the hope he could put that life behind him, but as is so often the case fate had intervened and in O'Reilly's case his stars were not aligned like everybody else's and his was a life where death and depravity could crop up at any time. That's just the way it was, and he was powerless to do anything about it.

"Time to hit the road," he said and finished what was left in his mug. "I think I'll take the car today – the wind is howling out there."

"That's probably why Bram didn't want to go outside," Assumpta said.

"He's spoilt. That fat beast is far too spoilt."

"He's stubborn, that's all. He's a lot like his owner."

"Stupid, more like. See if you can teach him how to use the cat flap. He's a cat – he ought to be able to figure out a cat flap."
"He will. What time will you be home?"
"Not late," O'Reilly looked at his watch. "I'd better be off. See what you can do with the cat."
"I will, Dad."

The crash of glass was followed by an almighty shriek from Bram. The ginger tom came running into the kitchen, made a beeline for the cat flap and darted outside.
"What the hell was that?" O'Reilly said.

He went through to the living room. Assumpta followed behind him. The brick was lying on the sofa that Bram had recently vacated. The glass in the window had withstood the force of the blow relatively well but there was a brick-sized hole smack bang in the middle of the pane. O'Reilly looked outside but there was nobody around. The gusting wind was throwing the branches of the trees back and forth outside the window. O'Reilly ran to the front door and opened it wide. He was hit with the full force of a forty-knot easterly. There was nobody out there. The sound of a car engine starting up could be heard over the howl of the wind. O'Reilly ran down the road and caught sight of a black car driving away at full pelt. It was too far away to make out the model or the registration number.

O'Reilly went back inside the apartment and found Assumpta inside the living room bent over the brick. It had landed in Bram's favourite spot on the sofa. O'Reilly forgot all forensics protocol and picked it up with his bare hands. There was something wrapped round the brick. It was a sheet of black paper tied on with thin rope. O'Reilly undid the knot and placed the paper on the coffee table. At the top something was written in white.
"What does it say?" Assumpta asked.
"*Have you missed me, Smiley*?" O'Reilly read.

"What does that mean?"

"I have no idea," O'Reilly replied but when he saw what had been drawn at the bottom of the page in red chalk, he could feel bile rising in his throat.

It was a symbol he recognised. It had been a very long time since he'd last seen it, but it had been such a prominent feature in his nightmares, he would never forget what the image on the black paper was supposed to represent.

Inside a circle was a crude drawing of a snake coiled around the neck of a stick drawing of a person. O'Reilly knew the stick figure was a woman even though it was only the long strands of hair on either side of the head that suggested this. He knew it was a woman because this was exactly the same chalk drawing that had been left on the doorsteps of four brutally murdered women in Dublin fifteen years ago. Each time there had been a number at the bottom of the chalk drawings – a number representing the order in which these women had been killed.

"Patrick Finney," O'Reilly said in a voice barely louder than a whisper. Assumpta looked at him. "The serial killer?"

"That symbol was his calling card."

"I remember reading something about him. Why would someone throw a brick through your window with Finney's calling card on it?"

"I really don't know."

Patrick Finney had succeeded in murdering four women before he was caught. It was one of the most high-profile cases in Irish history and one that O'Reilly would never forget. He was the man responsible for bringing Finney down.

And now someone had thrown a brick through his window with a drawing of Finney's calling card on a piece of paper attached to it. This wasn't the most disturbing aspect – at the bottom of the chalk drawing was another number. Bigger than the ones O'Reilly could remember it was a figure that chilled him to the bone.

Written in thick red chalk was the number – *5*.

CHAPTER TWO

O'Reilly had to concentrate hard during the short drive to work. The strong winds were making it difficult to steer and every now and then a gust would cause his car to veer off onto the other side of the road. The image on the piece of paper attached to the brick thrown through his window was still fresh in his mind. He'd asked Assumpta to get hold of a glazier to replace the pane of glass in the window. That wasn't the problem - windows could be replaced, but the message on the paper and the sketch drawn on it made O'Reilly feel sick to the stomach.

He'd put Patrick Finney out of his mind a long time ago. Finney was a depraved individual and O'Reilly had never met anyone like him before. For four months he held the city of Dublin in the grip of terror. Always killing by the light of the full moon and leaving behind nothing but the bizarre chalk drawing it seemed like he would never be caught. But he made a mistake with his fourth and final victim. He killed one of O'Reilly's colleagues. DC Ellie Finch was also a close friend of O'Reilly's and when her disfigured body was found it became personal. O'Reilly worked night and day to put together a picture of the man – it almost cost him his marriage and his sanity, but finally in the early hours of a cold September morning he stumbled across something that finally led him to the most disturbed killer Ireland had ever seen.

During the lengthy trial Finney spoke openly about his motivation for the murders. Intelligent and articulate he was like no killer O'Reilly had ever met before. He made it quite clear from the onset that he was quite prepared to keep on taking lives until he was caught. For him the full moon deserved sacrifice and it was his responsibility to offer these sacrifices. His defence had tried to persuade him to go the insanity route but Finney had vehemently ignored them and, in the end, he was sentenced to life in the most notorious prison in Ireland. Life without the possibility of parole.

And now the chalk drawing on the brick thrown through O'Reilly's window had brought everything back. O'Reilly didn't know what it meant, but he knew something sinister was afoot.

He parked in the car park at the station and got out of the car. The wind was showing no sign of dying down and he had to walk with his head bowed as he made his way to the entrance.

There was some kind of commotion by the front desk when O'Reilly came inside. A middle-aged woman was shouting at DS Will Skinner and it was clear from the detective sergeant's facial expression he didn't know how to handle it. O'Reilly walked over to them and the stench of stale alcohol hit his nostrils. The woman was clearly drunk but her accent was unmistakable. It was the unique brogue of east Dublin.

"What's going on?" O'Reilly asked DS Skinner.

The woman turned around and O'Reilly realised she was vaguely familiar.

"Long time, Smiley," she said and revealed a set of brown, jagged teeth.

O'Reilly recoiled at her foul breath. "What seems to be the problem?"

"Yer man here is the problem, Smiley," the woman said. "He's not taking me seriously."

"Will?" O'Reilly said to DS Skinner.

"Mrs O'Connell came to report an incident of assault," the red-faced DS said.

"Sexual assault," Mrs O'Connell elaborated. "And this one isn't believing me. I might be an old sot but it doesn't give 'em the right to use me, does it?"

O'Reilly was finding this hard to take in. He still couldn't remember where he'd seen this repulsive drunk woman before.

"I asked her about the alleged assault," DS Skinner said.

"There's nothing alleged about it," Mrs O'Connell said.

"And she told me she couldn't remember when it happened," DS Skinner said. "Or who it was that assaulted her."
"I know when I've been used," Mrs O'Connell said. "What are the Police going to do about it?"
"There's not much we can do about it if you can't remember anything about it," O'Reilly said in a calm voice.
"You haven't changed, Smiley," Mrs O'Connell said. "You can take the bastard out of the Gardai but you can't take the Gardai out of the bastard."
"Do I know you?" O'Reilly asked her.
"I know you, Smiley. I'll take my problems somewhere else then. Perhaps the Coast Guard can help."

She started to laugh and a chronic coughing fit followed. O'Reilly was worried she was going to throw up. The stench of her breath was getting unbearable. Without saying anything further she turned around and limped out of the station.

"She was a strange one," DS Skinner said. "Do you know her?"
"Her face rang a bell, but I could be wrong," O'Reilly said.
"Well, she seemed to know you."
"She's from Dublin – I was pretty well known back there."
"I don't doubt it, sir. What was all that *Smiley* stuff about?"
"Smiley O'Reilly," the Irish DI mused. "It was a bad attempt at sarcasm that seemed to stick. I was a bit of a cantankerous bastard back in Dublin."
"I'm glad you said it, sir," DS Skinner dared.

The two DCs Katie Owen and Andy Stone came in together. DC Stone looked even worse than he usually did. His rat-like eyes were bloodshot and his nose was red.
"Good God, Andy," O Reilly said. "You look worse than you normally do."
"I've got a nasty cold, sir," DC Stone said. "It's a change of season thing. I can feel a change of season is on the way."

"It's late September," O'Reilly reminded him. "Of course a change of season is on the cards. Morning Katie."
"Morning sir. What's the plan of action for today?"
"I need to check my emails," O'Reilly told her. "I'm waiting on some info from a source. I'll keep you in the loop."

He walked off down the corridor and bumped into Superintendent Anne Hayes on the way.
"Morning Liam," she said. "Anything new with these container robberies?"
"Morning, Ma'am," O'Reilly said. "I'm just waiting for some info from a source, and Jim promised me the forensic report from the latest one sometime this morning. I'll liaise with the DCI when I know more. How are things going there? With the wedding plans, I mean?"

Superintendent Hayes and DCI Tom Fish were engaged to be married. They'd managed to iron out a few problems along the way – the relationship between a superintendent and a detective chief inspector could have caused trouble at work but the Chief Constable had decided to offer his blessing and now Superintendent Hayes and DCI Fish were due to get married in a couple of weeks' time.

"Everything is going surprisingly smoothly," she said. "Tom agreed I would handle the majority of the planning."
"Probably for the best," O'Reilly said. "I'll keep you informed of any new developments."

He booted up the laptop in his office and switched on the kettle to make some tea while it was warming up. The howling wind outside was still raging. Every now and then a gust would rattle the window pane. O'Reilly thought back to the brick thrown through his window. The chalk drawing on the paper attached to the brick was definitely the same one left at the scenes of Patrick Finney's murders but O'Reilly still couldn't figure out the significance of the drawing here on the island. He wondered if someone was trying to wind him up. The case had been extremely high-profile and photographs of Finney's calling card had been plastered all over the newspapers. O'Reilly's name had also been in the papers for weeks. He hoped and prayed this was just the work of a sick-minded prankster and not something more sinister.

He turned his attention to his emails. He smiled when he saw he'd received a message from his source. He'd never met the woman – she insisted they communicate via email, but she'd proven to be very reliable in the short space of time she'd been helping him. The email was brief and straight to the point as always. It consisted of two names and an address. O'Reilly memorised the information, emailed a short thank you back then deleted her email. The address he'd been given meant a trip across the island to the affluent suburb of Vazon and O'Reilly wondered how someone who lived in Vazon could be involved in the theft of stock from a container in the capital.

There was no email from DI Peters yet. The Head of Forensics hadn't sent him the initial forensic on the latest robbery.

"That can wait," O'Reilly said and closed down his emails.

He leaned back in his chair and sipped his tea. The theft of some stock from containers down in the port wasn't urgent as far as he was concerned. The goods were no doubt insured and he wasn't going to stress too much over it.

His mobile phone started to ring in his jacket pocket. He took it out and saw it was a Dublin number.

He answered it. "O'Reilly."

"Liam," a familiar voice said. "It's DCI Mulligan."

"DCI?"

"I know, I still can't get used to it myself."

DCI Mulligan was a woman O'Reilly had worked closely with for almost fifteen years. When he left the Special Detective Unit six months ago, she held the same rank as him.

"A lot seems to have happened since I left," he said. "Congratulations."
"Thanks, Liam," she said. "But I'm afraid this isn't a social call."
"Go on."
"We've just got word from Portlaoise that Paddy Finney went over the walls last week."
"You're having me on?" O'Reilly couldn't believe what he was hearing.

Portlaoise Prison was the prison with possibly the highest security measures in Ireland. During the 1970s and 1980s it housed some of the most notorious IRA members and other paramilitary prisoners and the unique security measures it had in place made it almost impossible to escape from.
But Patrick Finney had somehow managed it.

"You said Finney escaped last week?" O'Reilly said. "Why wasn't I informed sooner?"
"Because they've only just realised he's gone."
"How the hell can that be possible? Portlaoise never drops the ball like that."
"It has now," DCI Mulligan said. "Finney was complaining of stomach problems and a burst appendix was suspected. He was taken to hospital in Kilkenny under armed guard. They feared they were too late – Finney managed to fool them he was at death's door and he was allowed a visit from his brother to say his goodbyes."

O'Reilly guessed the rest. "And this visit was unsupervised I suppose?"
"Right. You know how alike the Finney brothers are. Michael switched places with Patrick and nobody was any the wiser."
"And when they discovered Patrick's brother in the hospital bed, Patrick was long gone?"
"They only realised what had happened this morning when they were about to escort Finney back to Portlaoise. I phoned you as soon as I heard. I

thought about what Finney said to you when he was marched away that day in the courthouse."

Maybe I'll come and pay you a visit when I'm out.

O'Reilly remembered it too.

"I very much doubt he'll come anywhere near you," DCI Mulligan said. "It'll be far too risky and he'll know we'll be anticipating it, but I just wanted to warn you anyway."

"I appreciate it," O'Reilly said. "You're probably right - Finney would be stupid to risk approaching me."

They said their goodbyes and O'Reilly rubbed his eyes. He still couldn't believe what was happening. Patrick Finney had escaped and O'Reilly knew instinctively that a brick through the window was only just the start. Things were about to get a lot worse.

CHAPTER THREE

The container depot in St Peter Port was being battered by the elements. Gusting wind was rushing through the corridors between the metal containers and the waves were beating the harbour walls with a vengeance. O'Reilly and DC Katie Owen got out of the car and headed towards the admin office. A shiny red Porsche was parked close to the entrance. It had no registration plates and was clearly straight out of the box.

"I thought this kind of weather didn't happen in Guernsey." O'Reilly had to shout over the din of the wind.

"The easterly is the worst on this side of the island," DC Owen shouted back. "There'll be a calm after today – it's a full moon tonight and the wind usually dies down after a full moon. It'll be quite calm over in Vazon too."

"We're heading over there after this. I just want to speak to someone about a couple of people I've been given the names of."

"Where do you get your information from?"

"You don't need to know that, Katie. Let's get inside before this wind rips the skin off my face."

O'Reilly closed the door behind him and he and DC Owen walked up to the front desk.

O'Reilly took out his ID and showed it to the man behind the counter. "DI O'Reilly. We need to speak to someone in charge."

The man took a closer look at the warrant card. "O'Reilly? Irish?"

"There's no fooling you, is there? Can you point me in the direction of someone who runs this place?"

"You're looking at him. Bernard Harris. What can I do for you? I assume this is about the recent thefts?"

"That's right. I was wondering if you knew of someone by the name of James Locke?"

"He used to work here."

O'Reilly nodded. "What about Steven Banner?"

"Steve worked here too."

"When was this?"

"They both left at round about the same time. About two weeks ago."

"I see. And can you tell me why they left?"

"They didn't exactly leave," Bernard scratched his nose. "They were both fired."

"At the same time?" DC Owen asked. "Why were they both sacked at the same time?"

"What's this all about?" Bernard said.

"Please just answer the question," O'Reilly said.

"Jimmy and Steve weren't exactly what you would call model employees. They both worked out front – driving forklifts and unloading, and they were caught helping themselves to some of the goods in the containers."

"What sort of goods are we talking about?"

"Nothing major," Bernard replied. "Small stuff, but they were sacked on the spot when they were caught. Do you think they have something to do with the recent thefts?"

"It's possible," O'Reilly told him. "We won't take up anymore of your time."

"They share a house over in Vazon," Bernard said.

"Thanks," O'Reilly said and then thought of something. "Who owns that red Porsche outside?"

"I bought it a couple of weeks ago. It's a Panamera twin turbo 2.9. I got the four-wheel-drive model so I can go off road a bit. It's a dream to drive. It's a four-door but it's still a Porsche at heart."

O'Reilly didn't care too much about cars. He knew very little about them, but he did know the red car outside was probably very expensive.

"How much do those things go for?" he came out with it.

"The basic model is just under sixty grand but I paid a few grand more for the four-wheel-drive."
"They must pay well here," DC Owen joined in.
"You're joking, right? I never would have been able to get a Panamera on what they pay me here – I recently came into a large inheritance. I'm single, my house is paid off so I decided to spoil myself."
"Good for you," O'Reilly said. "We won't take up any more of your time."

"I know that look," DC Owen said as they drove away from the docks.
"What look?" O'Reilly said.
"You didn't believe Mr Harris back there, did you? You didn't buy his story about paying for the Porsche with an inheritance?"
"You're getting cynical, Katie," O'Reilly said. But, no I didn't believe him. Who in their right mind spends over sixty grand on a toy like that? You inherit that kind of money and you invest it."
"You think he has something to do with the recent thefts, don't you?"
"It did cross my mind. He calls the shots back there – he has access to the manifests and he knows exactly what's in every container. If anyone has the opportunity to carry out the thefts it's someone like Bernard Harris. We'll head over to Vazon to speak to the ex-employees but the Porsche man is right up there near the top of my list."

DC Owen had been right about the weather in Vazon. The wind was nowhere near as strong on the west of the island. James Locke and Steven Banner rented a small apartment in a complex three streets back from the golf course. When O'Reilly first came to the island, he couldn't get used to the nuisance of the security in these apartment complexes but they were quite familiar to him now. He stopped in front of the boom gate and waited for someone to come out of the small office next to it.

Nobody did. After thirty seconds or so O'Reilly opened the car door and got out.

"Anybody here?" he shouted.

He peered inside the security office, but it was empty. He looked down at the boom gate, took hold of the end and raised it into the air. He got back in the car and drove through before the boom gate dropped down again. In his rear-view mirror O'Reilly could see someone standing next to the gate. It was a man – his hands were in the air, and he was shouting something O'Reilly couldn't hear.

"He's going to moan at us when we come back out," DC Owen said.

"Let him, Katie," O'Reilly said. "I couldn't give a monkey's. Look out for apartment 22B."

They found it right at the end of the road. It was a small two-bedroomed place without a view of the sea or the golf course.

"These are the cheaper apartments, sir," DC Owen said. "They were the first ones to be built but when the bigger apartments were erected in front of them, they went down in price."

"It looks like someone's at home," O'Reilly parked next to a black Ford. "You can hear the music from out here."

After ringing the bell four times and getting no reply O'Reilly tried the door handle. The door was open. The music coming from inside was the type O'Reilly hated. The drum and bass was starting to give him a headache.

"Police," he shouted.

Nothing happened. The music seemed to be getting louder.

"Police," O'Reilly shouted again, louder this time.

A man who looked to be in his mid-twenties appeared from a doorway further down the hallway. He looked at O'Reilly and frowned.

"Mr Locke?" O'Reilly guessed. "Can we have a word?"

The man walked up to him. "What do you want?"

"Could you turn that racket off?" O'Reilly asked him. "We're from the Island Police and we need to talk to you."

It transpired O'Reilly had guessed wrongly – the man in the apartment wasn't James Locke, he was Locke's flatmate, Steven Banner. He'd reluctantly turned off the dreadful music and he was now sitting opposite O'Reilly and DC Owen in the small living room.

"What do you want?" he asked again.

"Where is Mr Locke?" O'Reilly said.

"How should I know? We're flatmates, we're not married."

The way his eyes were focused on anything but O'Reilly, coupled with his defensive attitude made the experienced Irish detective suspicious straight away. Steven Banner had something to hide.

"You used to work at the container depot over in the capital, didn't you?" O'Reilly said.

"What of it?" Steven said.

"Why did you leave?"

"Something better came along."

"I see. It's Monday morning, Mr Banner and I can't help noticing you're not at work."

"I meant I'm waiting for something better to come along. Do you think I want to be a forklift truck driver for the rest of my life?"

"Probably not."

"Mr Locke also worked with you, didn't he?" DC Owen said. "And he left at the same time. Is Mr Locke waiting for something better to come along too?"

"What exactly is it you want?" Steven said. "Is this about the thefts in the port? I read about it in the papers. If that's why you're here, you're wasting your time. I can tell you that right now."

"You and Mr Locke were fired, weren't you?" O'Reilly came out with it. "You were sacked on the spot because you were caught helping yourself to stock from the containers."

"Who told you that?" Steven said.

"That doesn't matter. Is it true?"
"Me and Jimmy nicked a couple of watches," Steven admitted. "That's all. They were fake Rolex things and they probably only cost a few quid to bring in."
"Are you telling me you lost your jobs because of a couple of Chinese rip-off watches?" DC Owen said.
"It was stupid, but Harris was adamant."
"Bernard Harris?"
"That's right. Thinks he's the bollocks because he's got money."
"Inheritance money?"
"That's what he reckons," Steven said. "But if you ask me, I reckon it's strange that as soon as these robberies begin Harris suddenly has a load of cash to spend. Have you seen that stupid car of his? If you're going to get a Porsche you get a Porsche. A two-door job that sits close to the ground. You don't get a four-door saloon or one of those stupid 4x4 things all the rich mothers drive their kids to school in."

O'Reilly realised they were getting side-tracked. "Mr Banner, I need to ask you where you were on these dates."
He listed the times and dates when the container thefts had occurred. Steven Banner smiled at him and O'Reilly knew they were probably about to rule him out of the investigation.
"Hold on," Steven left the room and returned with something in his hand. He handed it to O'Reilly.
O'Reilly read the ticket stub. "This is a return to Nice."
"Look at the dates," Steven said.
O'Reilly did. "According to this you flew out on Monday 10th of this month and returned a week later."
"Jimmy was with me," Steven said. "So that means we weren't even on the island when three of the robberies took place."

"Can I see?" DC Owen said.

O'Reilly handed her the stubs.

"There's no name on here," DC Owen said. "This doesn't prove anything."

"But a whole load of credit card slips and some Facebook posts of me and Jimmy in the South of France will, won't it?" Steven said.

"We'll be sure to check," O'Reilly said even though he knew Steven Banner was telling the truth.

The two men were eight hundred miles away in Nice at the times of three of the robberies.

"If I were you," Steven said as O'Reilly and DC Owen were about to leave. "I'd look more closely at Harris. That bastard isn't what he appears to be – you mark my words."

CHAPTER FOUR

After enduring a five-minute lecture from the security guard on the gate at the apartment complex, O'Reilly and DC Owen drove back to the other side of the island.

"I felt like I was back at school," DC Owen said. "That security guard was just like my old History teacher."

"He was an anally retentive prat," O'Reilly said. "People take security positions for one reason and one reason only – they crave the feeling of power it gives them. They're generally totally inept in their personal lives."

"Does that include the Police?" she said drily.

"It most definitely does, Katie. We're born losers, all of us."

"What now, sir?" DC Owen asked.

"Bernard Harris," O'Reilly replied. "I told you he's at the top of my list."

"Find out where the money for the Porsche actually came from, you mean?"

"It'll be easy to check. If he did really inherit it, he'll be more than willing to show us some proof, but I want to do a bit of digging before we speak to him again."

"To gain the upper hand?"

"Exactly." He glanced at his rear-view mirror. "That black car has been with us since we left Vazon."

They were now almost halfway across the island.

DC Owen tilted her head and looked in the passenger side mirror. "He's probably going the same way as us, sir."

"Let's make sure, shall we?"

O'Reilly turned left off Le Villocq and headed for Le Friquet Garden Centre. He looked in the mirror and realised the black car was still behind them. He turned right then right again and drove through the Memorial Gardens back onto Le Villocq.

"He's still there, Katie," O'Reilly said. "We're being followed."
"Why would someone follow us?"
"I don't know. I'm going to stop and see what he does."

He indicated and turned right into the car park of the St Pierre Park Hotel. The black car sped off down Le Villocq.
"What's going on, sir?" DC Owen asked.
O'Reilly decided to tell her about the incident at home that morning.
"Someone threw a brick threw my window this morning. It gave my poor cat a heart attack. At first I thought it was probably just someone causing a bit of malicious damage but there was a note attached to the brick."
"What did it say?"
"Are you missing me, Smiley," O'Reilly remembered. "That's not what's worrying me. Have you heard of a man by the name of Patrick Finney?"
"The name rings a bell."
"It was before your time, but fifteen years ago Finney murdered four women in Dublin. He killed one a month by the light of the full moon. The last one was a good friend of mine and then it became personal. I had to catch him. I worked night and day – I nearly ended up with a divorce because of it but one night I realised he'd slipped up. He'd left something behind at the last one and that's what led me to him. I was the one who stopped him. He was sentenced to life without parole."
"That must have been terrible for you," DC Owen said. "Losing one of your friends like that."
"He's out, Katie," O'Reilly said. "I got word this morning from an old colleague that he jumped the walls last week. Finney is on the loose and I think he's coming for me."

Neither of them spoke for a while. Both of them stared out of the window at the hotel in front of them.

"When I ran outside this morning after the brick was thrown," O'Reilly said. "I saw a black car racing away. It was too far away to make out the model but I'm sure it's the same car that followed us from Vazon."
"He'd be taking a huge risk coming to the island," DC Owen said. "Surely he'll be aware the Police will be on the lookout for him here?"
"Paddy Finney isn't a normal, rational human being, Katie. He's a monster and he's a devious bastard to boot. He's a natural charmer and he seems to have an ability to make people do things. He gained access to all four victims with this charm. Including my friend and colleague. I think he's coming for me."
"You have to let the Super know."
"I'm afraid that won't help, Katie. I'm going to have to deal with this on my own. I know how Finney operates and the brick and the black car tailing me was Finney trying to rattle me. I'll not be rattled by the likes of him. I'll keep my ears and eyes open and I'll know it if something's wrong. I'd appreciate it if you could keep this to yourself for the time being."
"Of course," DC Owen said. "It was a Toyota Yaris by the way."
"What?"
"The car that was following us was a Toyota Yaris if that's any help."
O'Reilly smiled. "Thanks, Katie. Let's get going, shall we?"

* * *

They didn't see the black Yaris again and O'Reilly wondered if the brick through the window that morning had made him unnecessarily paranoid. DS Andy Stone was smoking a cigarette outside in the car park at the station when they got there.
"Feeling better, Andy," O'Reilly asked him.
"Not really, sir," the rat-eyed DC replied.
"Perhaps you shouldn't be smoking," DC Owen said. "It can't be very good for you when you've got a cold."

"It's a filthy habit whether you've got a cold or not," O'Reilly said. "I need some tea inside me then we've got a suspect to look into."

"Suspect?" DC Stone took the cigarette out of his mouth and stared at it. It had gone out.

"Bernard Harris," DC Owen told him. "He's some kind of foreman at the port. He bought himself a Porsche Panamera a couple of weeks ago. That was the same time the robberies started."

"A Panamera?" DC Stone flicked his lighter but the flame kept going out in the strong wind. "That's not a proper Porsche."

"It's a sixty grand car," O'Reilly said. "Now stop trying to light that disgusting thing. Briefing room in twenty. I need to get some tea inside of me first."

CHAPTER FIVE

Assumpta sipped her coffee, leaned back in her chair and smiled. She'd just finished re-reading her article on two of the island's longest residents and she was extremely pleased with it. The Durand and the Simon families had been on the island for longer than any other and the feud that had developed between the two was legendary in Guernsey. For decades the two clans had been at loggerheads and it had all come to a head earlier in the year when the age-old fight culminated in murder. The shocking truth about the Durands and the Simons had come to the surface and for one of the Durands, it had been all too much. Arno Durand couldn't take it anymore and he'd locked himself in his study one night and wasn't seen for more than two days. He was found by his son, Desmond with a bullet through his temple. The gun was still in his hand.

Assumpta knew she had to take this tragedy into account when she wrote her story – no matter what the Durand family were responsible for she still needed to respect the fact they had suffered a great loss, and the end product was an article she was extremely proud of. She ran a final spell check and emailed the piece to her editor at the Guernsey Gazette. Assumpta knew Fiona would love it and she'd barely stirred the milk into a fresh cup of coffee when her phone started to ring on the kitchen counter.

Assumpta saw from the screen it was Fiona.

She answered the call. "That was quick."

"I just did a quick skim read," Fiona said. "But from what I read it looks brilliant. As usual. Did you see the crap the Herald put on their online site last night?"

"I had a quick look through," Assumpta took a sip of her coffee.

"It was absolute drivel. They all but glamorised Arno's suicide. It was disgusting."

"Nothing surprises me where Fred the Ed is concerned," Assumpta said.

The sound of the doorbell could be heard.

"I have to go," Assumpta said. "There's somebody at the door. It's probably the glazier."

"Glazier?" Fiona asked.

"I'll tell you all about it later."

"That latest article of yours is brilliant," Fiona said once more. "I'm going to have to watch you – you'll be snapped up by the New York Times if you keep putting out stuff like this."

Assumpta laughed. "Not likely. I'll see you later."

She rang off and went to answer the door. The wind had died down a bit and the sun had come out. There was nobody there. Assumpta stepped outside and spotted a small package on the doorstep. She looked around but there was nobody to be seen. She picked up the small box and read the label. It was handwritten and all that was written on it was her father's name. Liam O'Reilly – that was it. There was no indication where the parcel had come from – there was no details of the sender and no postage stamp or post mark.

"Strange," Assumpta said and took the package back inside the apartment.

Bram was sitting by the cat flap in the kitchen when Assumpta came in. The ginger tom was staring at the flap in the bottom of the door.

"You know what to do," Assumpta bent down and opened the flap.

Bram remained where he was.

"When you want to go out you use your head and open it up. You managed it quite well when that brick came through the window earlier."

Bram didn't seem impressed. He rolled on his side and closed his eyes.

Assumpta came up with an idea. She opened the fridge and took out a tin of tuna. Bram was instantly alert – tuna was his favourite food. Assumpta emptied the tin into Bram's bowl, opened the back door and slipped through without letting Bram outside. She put the bowl down a few metres away from the door and waited. She didn't have to wait long – Bram's head appeared from the cat flap and soon the rest of him followed. The tuna was gone within a minute. While he was busy licking the bowl Assumpta went back inside the kitchen and closed the door behind her.

"If you want to come back in, you're going to have to use the cat flap," she said to the closed door.

The sound of her phone ringing cut short the cat flap training session. She picked it up and saw it was a number not in her contacts.

"Hello," she answered it.

"The brick was just the start," a man with a deep voice said.

That was it. The man didn't say anything more.

Assumpta looked at the phone and immediately knew something was terribly wrong. The sound of the man's voice had stirred up something inside her and she knew instinctively that something terrible was about to happen. Her mother, Mary had a kind of sixth sense as did her mother before her and Assumpta had inherited this rare talent. It was impossible to explain but the women in Mary's family had some kind of intuition that allowed them to sense things other people couldn't, and right now Assumpta sensed the man who had just called her was going to bring sadness and terror to her life.

She brought up O'Reilly's number and pressed, dial.

"Summi," O'Reilly answered immediately. "I was just about to head to a briefing. Can we talk later?"

"I think Patrick Finney just phoned me," Assumpta said.

O'Reilly didn't say anything.

"Dad," Assumpta said. "Are you still there?"

"I'm here. What did he say?"

"He said the brick was just the start."

"Where are you?"

"Still at home. I was trying to get Bram to use the cat flap when the phone rang. A strange package arrived for you too. It was just left outside on the doorstep. I'm sure it was Finney who phoned – I could sense something bad in his voice."

O'Reilly knew better than to doubt this. His years with Mary had taught him to take this sixth sense very seriously.

"I'm on my way. Lock the doors and keep your phone close. I'll be there in ten minutes."

He made it in five. He unlocked the door and went inside. Assumpta was in the living room with Bram on her lap. The cat had suddenly learned how to use the cat flap and hadn't left her side since she'd phoned her father.

"I need that number," O'Reilly said.

"It's still on my phone," Assumpta said. "I'm fine by the way."

"Sorry," O'Reilly said. "Was it a mobile number?"

"It was a landline. Probably a payphone."

"Probably," O'Reilly agreed.

"How did he get my number?"

"If we're assuming it's Finney, he has ways. He still knows people. You mentioned something about a package."

"It's in the kitchen. Bram's learned how to use the cat flap by the way."

"Grand," O'Reilly said and went through to the kitchen.

He picked up the small box, and looked at his name on the front. He couldn't be a hundred percent certain but he was sure the writing was the same as the writing on the note attached to the brick thrown through his window. The package wasn't very heavy. O'Reilly gave it a tentative shake, but nothing moved inside it. All of his detective instincts were telling him to hand the box over to forensics to let them analyse it but his curiosity was stronger than his intuition. He found a kitchen knife on the draining board and carefully slit open the tape that had been used to seal the box. He opened up one side and looked inside. He couldn't quite make out what it was so he started to open the other flap. Something was preventing him from doing so. Something was stuck to the tape. O'Reilly gave it a yank, there was a popping sound as the balloon inside burst and a cloud of dust exploded into O'Reilly's face and settled on the material of his jacket.

CHAPTER SIX

The phone used to call Assumpta turned out to be a payphone in Les Varendes. O'Reilly knew the phone call was a dead end. There would be no way to ascertain who used the phone at that particular time. One thing that O'Reilly did know was Les Varendes was a stone's throw from where he and DC Owen had parked to try and lose the car that had been following them. O'Reilly had no doubt in his mind that Patrick Finney was on the island and he also knew it was only a matter of time before he made his presence known and the Irish detective wasn't sure what he was going to do about it.

The contents of the package were still a mystery. When the balloon had popped O'Reilly's initial fear was it was some kind of toxin – a substance that was designed to do him harm but when nothing happened to him, he assumed the intention was simply to rattle him further. He'd changed his clothes and dumped the dust covered ones in the washing basket. He insisted on driving Assumpta to the offices of the Guernsey Gazette and now he was about to head up the briefing back at the station.

"Sorry about that." He decided not to mention the cause of his sudden departure from the station earlier. "Let's make a start, shall we? The names given to me by a usually reliable source have turned out to be a dead end. James Locke and Steven Banner can be ruled out for three of the robberies and as I firmly believe all the thefts were carried out by the same perpetrators, we can rule them out of the other one too. Locke and Banner were in the South of France at the time and credit card slips confirmed this."

"Sounds like your source isn't as reliable as you thought," DCI Tom Fish said.

DCI Fish had come to accept that O'Reilly would be the one heading up most of the investigations despite his inferior rank. Rank aside, Fish knew O'Reilly was by far the more experienced detective.

"She's never let me down in the past," O'Reilly said. "But I suppose you can't be right all the time. Katie and I spoke to the manager down at the container terminal earlier and something aroused my curiosity. Bernard Harris has recently purchased an extremely expensive car."

"A Porsche Panamera," DC Stone elaborated. "It's a ponce's Porsche."

"Thank you for that, Andy," O'Reilly said. "Whatever it is, it's straight out of the box and cost more than sixty thousand pounds. Mr Harris claims he's recently inherited a substantial amount of money and that'll be easy enough to find out about, but I want to do some digging around in his life before we speak to him about it."

"What for?" DC Stone asked. "We find out he inherited the money for the gay Porsche he's off the hook."

O'Reilly glared at him. "I will have none of that talk from anyone on my team, Andy. We look further into his life because there's something bothering me about Bernard Harris."

"Besides the fact he's bought a girl's car?" DC Stone clearly wasn't quite finished.

"I got the impression he's hiding something," O'Reilly said. "I could be wrong."

"He's in charge down at the depot," DC Owen added. "He deals with the manifests and he knows the details of everything that comes in and out of the port."

"We know for a fact that the containers that were targeted were particularly lucrative ones as far as a robbery is concerned. Whoever robbed these containers knew exactly what was inside them."

"The first two were electrical goods," DCI Fish elaborated. "And the second two were consignments of mobile phones. All of which can be converted into cash relatively quickly."

"I'm not suggesting it was Bernard Harris who physically carried out the robberies," O'Reilly said. "But I get the feeling he's involved somehow."

"How, exactly?" DS Skinner asked.

"I'm not sure. It could be he tips off the robbers about what containers to hit, and when exactly to do so, or it could be something else, but the man is involved in this."

"Let's look into him then," DCI Fish said. "Katie, I want you and Andy to check out his history. See if anything jumps out at you."

DC Stone didn't even try and hide his irritation. He sighed so loudly it was difficult to miss.

"Is something wrong, Andy?" O'Reilly asked him.

"I just don't see why we're going to so much trouble for a few robberies. Nobody got hurt and the goods they nicked will be insured."

"Because they've broken the law, that's why. And we cannot have people breaking the law, can we?"

"Liam," DCI Fish said. "Speak with your source again. See if he's heard anything about large quantities of stolen goods being offered for sale."

"She, sir," O'Reilly said. "My source is a woman."

"Speak to her."

"She was way off the mark with the two names she gave us," DC Stone reminded them.

"Perhaps she wasn't," O'Reilly thought out loud.

"They were in the South of France when three of the containers were hit," DS Skinner said.

"But it doesn't rule them out altogether. We've overlooked the possibility they could be involved in the distribution of the stolen goods. My source wouldn't have offered their names without good reason."

"Steven Banner did seem like he was hiding something," DC Owen said. "And it was odd how smug he got when he gave us his alibi. You don't act like that unless you've done something wrong and got away with it."

"We'll speak to Banner again," O'Reilly said. "And we need to see if we can get hold of his flatmate, James Locke."

"Let's get going then," DCI Fish said. "Liam, can I have a word in private?"

"What's up?" O'Reilly asked DCI Fish when the rest of the team had left the briefing room.

"Patrick Finney."

The DCI's two words made O'Reilly flinch.

"What about him?" he asked.

"He's escaped."

"I am aware of that."

"And we've been warned he could be heading this way."

"We?" O'Reilly said.

"Superintendent Hayes told me about it. She had a phone call from Ireland. How did you find out about Finney's escape from prison?"

"An old colleague of mine called this morning to let me know," O'Reilly said. "She thought I should know."

"And you didn't think to inform anyone else about this?"

"What for? Finney is hardly likely to show up somewhere that he knows everyone is looking for him," O'Reilly said.

"You don't sound too convinced, Liam. I'm not a fool. Has something happened? Has Finney made contact with you?"

"I don't know," O'Reilly realised how stupid he sounded as soon as the words left his mouth.

"What's going on?"

"I think Finney is trying to put the wind up me. Things have been happening. There's nothing I can link directly to Finney, but I'm sure he's behind it."

"What kind of things?"

"Someone threw a brick through my window this morning," O'Reilly told him. "Then I got the feeling someone was following me on the way back from Vazon. My daughter received a phone call telling her the brick was just the start and someone sent me a package with nothing in it but a balloon and a load of dust."

"A balloon full of dust?"

"I know," O'Reilly said. "I have no idea what it means, but someone is trying to rattle my cage."

"By someone you mean Patrick Finney?"

"Paddy Finney doesn't scare me, sir," O'Reilly said. "He didn't back then and he doesn't now. I'll handle it."

"That's what I'm afraid of. If anything else happens I want to be the first to know. Have you got that?"

"Loud and clear, sir. Will that be all? We've got a lot to get through."

"Do not handle this on your own, Liam."

"I'll bear that in mind. How are things going with the wedding plans?"

"I've left that up to Anne and she's quite happy for my involvement to consist of nothing more than me turning up on the day. Everybody wins."

"Have you organised a stag do?"

"I don't think that's a good idea."

"It's a grand idea. I can help you out there if you like."

"Thanks for the offer, but I think I'll pass. I'm getting a bit long in the tooth for that kind of thing."

"Nonsense," O'Reilly said. "You're never too old for a pre-nuptial knees-up."

"I think I'll give it a miss. Thanks, but no thanks."

"Let me know if you change your mind."

CHAPTER SEVEN

O'Reilly had barely made it outside to the carpark when his phone started to ring. He took it out, looked at the screen and smiled.

"Victoria," he answered it. "It's grand to hear from you."

Victoria Radcliffe was a woman O'Reilly had been in a relationship with for a few months. She and her brother owned a motorcycle shop in Vazon and hers and O'Reilly's was an unusual match. O'Reilly still couldn't for the life of him figure out what a beautiful woman like Victoria saw in a grumpy old Irish detective like him.

"What are you up to later?" she asked him.

"Nothing as yet," he replied.

"I know it's Monday, but do you feel like going out for a meal?"

"I'd love to. Your side of the island or mine?"

Victoria started to laugh. "You make it sound like we own the place. I'll come to you. Let's say the Red Snapper at seven?"

"Seven it is then. I'll look forward to it."

As O'Reilly drove back to Vazon he realised he had a huge grin on his face. The phone call from Victoria had made him forget about everything else. They'd only been together for a relatively short space of time but in that time, they'd grown closer and closer and O'Reilly still felt like a teenager at times when he was around her.

He was on his way to speak to Steven Banner again, and he hoped that this time James Locke would also be home. He realised he'd taken his eyes off the ball earlier when he and DC Owen spoke to Banner – the fact that he and Locke were in France when three of the robberies were carried out shouldn't have automatically discounted them from being involved and O'Reilly felt like an idiot for ruling them out. His source had never let him down in the past and there was no reason why she would start now.

The same security guard O'Reilly had upset earlier was still manning the front gate. O'Reilly held his ID out of the window and was surprised when he was let straight through without further ado. He parked in the same place as before. The black Ford was still there, as was a white van.

It was James Locke who answered the door this time. He was shorter and much stockier than James Banner but the smug grin on his face was exactly the same as his flatmate's.

"Mr Locke, I presume," O'Reilly said and took out his ID.

"Steve said you came round earlier," James said. "What do you want now?"

"Can I come inside?"

"Do I have a choice?"

"Not really."

Steven Banner was playing a game on an Xbox in the living room when O'Reilly came in with James.

"I see the jobhunting is going well," O'Reilly said.

"I'm taking a bit of time off," James didn't even look up from his game.

"Got a bit of cash stashed away, have you?"

"I do alright."

"Could you please turn that off? I need to speak to you."

"I thought I told you everything this morning."

"Turn that bloody game off," O'Reilly said.

Steven did as he was asked.

"What's this all about?" he said. "I already told you me and Jimmy were in Nice when three of the robberies took place.

"Yes, you were. I'm not here about that. Although it is very convenient for you."

"What are you talking about?" It was James Locke.

"Just thinking out loud. Is that your van parked outside?"

"What about it?"

"Is it your van or not?"

"It's mine," James said. "It's not illegal to own a van, is it?"

"Not as far as I'm aware. What do you use the van for?"

"This and that."

"Transporting stolen goods, perhaps?"

"What?"

"Still thinking out loud," O'Reilly said. "You won't mind if I have a look inside it, will you?"

"Have you got a warrant?" Steven asked.

"I can get one."

"Get one then," James said. "Until then you're not going anywhere near my van."

O'Reilly thought for a second.

"Here's what we're going to do," he said. "I'm going to take a look inside that van. What's going to happen is this: I'm going to take out my phone and call one of my colleagues. He can be here within ten minutes. Then the four of us are going to stay right where we are until the search warrant is organised."

"You can't do that," Steven said.

"Then," O'Reilly continued. "We'll rip that van apart. The only problem is the search warrant. It's time consuming, you see, but I have to be sure you won't go near the van and get rid of what's inside it."

This was a blatant lie. O'Reilly could obtain a search warrant – it would take some time, but he had no power to hold Banner and Locke while it was being authorised. He hoped their knowledge of the law was limited.

It was.

"I'll show you," James Locke stood up. "There's nothing in the van."

37

O'Reilly followed him outside and watched as James unlocked the van and opened the back doors wide. Apart from a couple of dirty overalls the back of the van was empty.

CHAPTER EIGHT

"You do realise you had no right to search that van," DCI Fish told O'Reilly back at the station.

"*He* didn't know that," O'Reilly argued.

"You know as well as I do you need reasonable grounds to carry out a search without a warrant."

"I told you, he didn't know that. I asked him to unlock the van and he obliged. No harm done."

"Thankfully not. Do you still think they're involved in this?"

"I do. They're in on it, and I think Bernard Harris is too. I'm starting to think Banner and Locke's dismissal from their jobs at the container terminal is connected."

"How do you mean?"

"They get fired then conveniently they have alibis for three of the robberies. It doesn't fit. They're involved."

"You're forgetting one thing, Liam," DCI Fish said. "If Bernard Harris didn't carry out the robberies nor did James Locke or Steven Banner, it means we're still looking for who did."

"This thing is more organised than we thought. What was the value of the goods that were stolen?"

"Around seven hundred thousand, give or take a few thousand."

"Then it's plausible that a fair-sized group of people are behind it. Even if there are six or seven of them it still means a hundred grand each. That's nothing to be sniffed at."

"Have you heard anything more to suggest that Patrick Finney is on the island?" DCI Fish changed the subject.

"Not a sausage," O'Reilly had put the whole thing out of his mind. "But I promise you, you'll be the first one to know if he shows up."

"Why don't I believe that? What's the story with you and Finney? I seem to recall the case back then but the details are a bit hazy."

"Paddy Finney killed four women back in the early 2000's," O'Reilly said. "From June to September he held the whole of Dublin in the grip of terror. He only killed when the moon was full and he chose his victims at random. His MO was different each time and that's why we couldn't catch him."

"*You* caught him, Liam," DCI Fish reminded him.

"He made a mistake," O'Reilly said. "And that mistake was killing one of my closest colleagues and friends. Ellie Finch was her name. She was a DC at the time and I was her DS. When Finney killed Ellie, he made it personal. I worked night and day and I didn't stop. I almost lost everything during those few weeks but I had to keep going. Then I got a breakthrough. Finney had left something behind at Ellie's house. I didn't see it at first because it didn't seem important but when I went through everything again late one September night it all fitted together."

"What did he leave behind?" DCI Fish asked.

"He got too big for his boots. Ellie had been working on the case notes and we found them on the desk in her living room, a few feet away from her body. We took them in but didn't pay them much attention. But something about them jumped out at me when I looked at them again that night. Parts of the investigation information had been crossed out in red pen. And when I looked more closely, I realised the bits that had been crossed out were the parts we'd been speculating about. It was stuff that wasn't factual. Hypotheses we'd been working on. The bastard crossed out the bits that were wrong and only left the bits that were actually relevant to the investigation. His mistake was leaving behind the pen he used."

"That's impressive detective work, Liam."

"I told you," O'Reilly said. "I refused to give up. We pulled a couple of prints from the pen. Finney had done some time back in the nineties, and his prints were on record. Four dead women and the only prints he left behind were at Ellie's place. He would have kept on killing until he was caught – he said so himself in court."

"Fifteen years is a long time," DCI Fish said. "Long enough time to plan revenge."

"That's a bit melodramatic, isn't it?"

"No, it's not. You need to be extremely careful, and if you get one whiff of Finney, you're to call it in. Is that understood?"

"I told you," O'Reilly said. "I'm hearing you loud and clear. I'm going to see what Katie and Andy have found out about Bernard Harris and then I'm going to pay the Porsche owner another visit."

He found the DCs Owen and Stone in the office they shared. DC Owen was looking at something on the screen of her laptop.

"Found anything?" O'Reilly asked her.

"It appears Mr Harris was telling the truth about the inheritance," she said. "His mother passed away six months ago."

"Just because his mother died doesn't mean he's suddenly become a wealthy man."

"There's more, sir. Juliette Harris was some kind of French legend. I've never heard of her before but she was quite famous in Paris back in her day. Then she was known as Juliette Moreau and she was a big name on the social scene. She married a TV producer – Bill Harris and they moved to the island just before Bernard was born. Bill passed away when Bernard was a teenager – he had no brothers or sisters so he was sole heir."

"How much money are we talking about?" O'Reilly asked.

"Not an awful lot in terms of socialites these days – Juliette liked to spend from what I read, but Bernard probably netted around a quarter of a million."

"And you think that's not a lot? Two-hundred-and-fifty grand?"

"More than enough to buy a useless Porsche," DC Stone joined in. "And have money left to spare. Bernard Harris had nothing to do with the robberies."

"Don't be so quick to jump to conclusions, Andy," O'Reilly said.

"He's loaded, sir," DC Stone said. "Why would he risk going to jail if he's already got more cash than all of us put together?"

"Stranger things have happened. What else do we know about the man?"

"His Facebook privacy settings are sky-high," DC Owen said. "So I couldn't see his activity on there, but I'm inclined to agree with Andy. Why would a man worth so much money risk everything by robbing the place where he works? Surely he would know he'd be under suspicion straight away?"

O'Reilly knew she had a valid point. Bernard Harris didn't need the money and if he was involved and caught out, he would be facing a lengthy prison term. O'Reilly wondered if he was off the mark with this one. His intuition had rarely let him down in the past but he was starting to think the business with Patrick Finney was starting to affect him more than he realised. It was preventing him from thinking straight and his decisions were no longer rational.

"What now, sir?" DC Owen asked.

"Forensics," O'Reilly said. "DI Peters ought to have something for us by now. Perhaps the perpetrators left something behind at the last one. I'll go and speak to him in person. In the meantime, take a break. Go and grab some lunch. If anything new comes to light I'll organise another briefing – if not, I'm wide open to any suggestions you have."

CHAPTER NINE

"Fifty grand," Delores O'Connell said for the third time in the space of a minute.

"I said thirty," Patrick Duncan Finney said. "Thirty grand, take it or leave it."

"Fifty grand isn't too much to ask for what you're wanting me to do."

Delores started to cough so violently a woman on the table next to the window turned and stared at her. Delores took out a handkerchief and coughed into it. She looked at the blood on the white handkerchief and stuffed it back inside her pocket.

"You're dying, Delores," Finney reminded her. "Thirty grand will see your family right for a while."

Delores looked at him with dead eyes. "Forty?"

"Thirty-five and we do it this evening. I promise it'll be quick and painless."

"Thirty-five then," Delores held out her hand.

Finney shook his head. "I don't think so, Delores. See you later. There'll be a full moon tonight. God, you don't know how much I've missed it."

Delores watched him walk away. He stopped by the table next to the window.

"Afternoon," he said to the woman sitting there. "Dreadful weather out there."

He smiled and the woman smiled back. Finney nodded and left the café. The woman's cheeks had flushed bright red.

* * *

"Graham Quinn," DI Jim Peters handed O'Reilly a piece of paper.

The Head of Forensics was grinning from ear to ear.

"He's in the system," Peters added. "Did a few months a while back for breaking and entering."

"Do we know anything else about him?" O'Reilly asked.

"You mean is he tied to the container depot in any way?"

"Right. If his prints were found inside the latest container that was hit, could they have got there by any other means?"

"That's your job, Liam," Peters said. "I'm just telling you what we found. Graham Quinn's prints were found on the locking mechanism and inside the container. I'll leave the rest up to you."

"Good work, Jim. At least we've got something to go on now."

"Are you alright?" Peters asked. "You seem a bit off."

"I've been worse," was all O'Reilly was willing to offer. "I'll round up the troops and we'll pay our Mr Quinn a visit."

He found DC Owen in the canteen. She was reading a book and didn't even realise he was standing next to her table. A half-eaten sandwich was on the table in front of her. DC Stone was nowhere to be seen.

"Good book?" O'Reilly said.

DC Owen looked up at him. "Sorry, sir. I was miles away there. It's an autobiography of Ellen MacArthur. She's a real inspiration. Did you know she was only twenty-eight when she sailed solo around the world? That's amazing, don't you think?"

"I'm not a big fan of boats, Katie. DI Peters has given us something to go on. The prints belonging to a man by the name of Graham Quinn were found on the latest container to be hit – inside and out. It could be he works down at the container port but we'll find out. I wanted to pay the Porsche man another visit today anyway. Where's Andy disappeared to?"

"He went outside for a smoke," she told him.

"Those things are going to kill him one day. Let's go and find him, shall we?"

The wind had died down slightly when they arrived at the port and O'Reilly was glad. If there was one thing he couldn't stand it was gusting winds.

"The pointless Porsche is still here," DC Stone pointed to the shiny red car.

"I can see that, Andy," O'Reilly said. "So, Mr Harris ought to still be at work."
"How are we going to play it?" DC Owen asked.
"Carefully. We inform Mr Harris that some new information has come to light and we need a list of everybody who works here. That's it. If Graham Quinn's name is on that list we've got a bit of a problem and if it isn't it's Mr Quinn with the problem. Let's go and see what Bernard Harris can tell us. And Andy?"
"Sir?" DC Stone said and sniffed loudly.
"Don't mention the Porsche."
"Why would I mention the Porsche?"
"I know you, and insulting the man's car right now isn't going to help anyone."

Bernard Harris didn't seem particularly bothered to see the three of them. O'Reilly walked straight up to the counter.
"Have you found something?" Bernard asked him.
"We think so," O'Reilly replied. "I'm going to need a list of everybody who works here – especially those who have access to the containers."
"Have you spoken to James and Steven?"
"More than once. Could you organise that list please?"

Bernard walked through a door behind him and returned a short time later with a single piece of paper.
"Everything's on here. Names, contact details -everything you need."
O'Reilly looked down the list. Graham Quinn's name wasn't on it.
"Are you sure this is everybody?"
"Everybody," Bernard confirmed. "Everybody from the office staff to the forklift drivers."
"What about people who no longer work here?" DC Owen said. "Do you have a list of those people?"
"Especially those who have left in the past month or so," O'Reilly added.

"I can tell you that myself," Bernard said. "There are two of them and I believe you've already spoken to them more than once."

O'Reilly didn't appreciate the smug grin on his face when he said this.

"Will there be anything else?" Bernard said. "We've got a consignment of toiletries that needs to be unloaded ASAP. It was supposed to have arrived on Friday but they ran into some trouble in the Red Sea. We need to get that container emptied today."

"I think that's everything," O'Reilly said. "We'll probably need to talk to you again."

DC Stone looked at Bernard and O'Reilly knew straight away he was going to mention the Porsche. He shook his head, but DC Stone didn't see him.

"I believe that's your Panamera outside?" the rat-faced DC said.

"She's a beauty, isn't she?" Bernard said.

"What's the top speed? It must weigh quite a bit more than a proper Porsche."

"It is a proper Porsche, and the claimed top speed is a little under two-hundred-miles per hour. Of course, there's not many places you can go that fast and I think I've only had her up to forty-five."

"I thought as much," DC Stone mumbled to himself.

CHAPTER TEN

"What part of *don't mention the Porsche* didn't you understand, Andy?" O'Reilly asked DC Stone.

They were on their way across the island. Graham Quinn rented an apartment halfway between King's Mills and Vazon. O'Reilly had dropped DC Owen off at the station.

"I just wanted to confirm what I already suspected," DC Stone said. "Why spend over sixty grand on car you're only going to drive at forty-five miles an hour?"

"It's the speed limit on most of the island," O'Reilly reminded him.

"If I had a car that could go that fast, I'd wind it up a bit. Bugger the speed limit."

"I'll pretend I didn't hear that. Graham Quinn has no connection to the container depot as far as we know, so how did his prints end up on the latest container to be hit? Will and Katie are busy looking for links between Quinn, James Locke and Steven Banner."

"What about connections to Bernard Harris? There's something dodgy about that man."

"I'm inclined to agree with you," O'Reilly turned left onto La Hurette. "But I'm beginning to suspect Mr Harris is no more than a source of info."

"What do you mean?"

"I reckon he just provides the intel. He knows what's in the containers and he knows when the depot is going to be quiet. I wouldn't be surprised if he has access to the security too. When you think about it it's quite ingenious. Let's say he takes a cut on the sale of the stolen goods – his hands are clean and there's nothing to link him to any of the robberies."

"One of the others could talk," DC Stone pointed out. "They could spill the beans about his involvement."

"That's what we're hoping we'll get out of Graham Quinn."

"How's Assumpta?" DC Stone said out of the blue. "I haven't seen her for a while."

I'd prefer it if you'd kept it that way, O'Reilly thought.

His daughter and DC Stone had hit it off from the word go. O'Reilly had tried to figure out what Assumpta saw in the shifty-eyed DC but so far, he couldn't think of anything that she could possibly find attractive. His repulsive appearance aside, he was moody, grumpy and prone to bouts of sulking. He smoked and his personal hygiene left a lot to be desired. All in all, he was a very unattractive man and O'Reilly couldn't for the life of him figure out what Assumpta saw in him.

"This is the place here," O'Reilly stopped the car outside.

He was relieved there was no security gate to get through.

"My Mum grew up around here," DC Stone said as they got out of the car. "Her parents had a place overlooking the nature reserve. Me and my brother used to go there a lot when we were kids."

"How's your dad getting on?" O'Reilly asked.

DC Stone's mother had died suddenly a short while ago. His father had found her in the bath and later it was confirmed she'd suffered a massive stroke.

"He's OK," DC Stone said. "He's handling it the only way he knows how – with the help of a beer or two. I'm starting to come to terms with it."

"Glad to hear it. Unfortunately, the Grim Reaper comes for us all sooner or later. It's unavoidable."

"Does Mr Quinn know we're here?"

"Where's the fun in that? No, I find it better to catch them unawares. I don't see any sports cars parked around here, so that's one less thing to worry about."

"A Porsche Panamera is not a sports car, sir," DC Stone said. "It's an overpriced vehicle for taking spoilt rich kids to school."

They walked up to the door and O'Reilly pressed the buzzer for number four.

"Who is it?" a man's voice was heard over the speaker shortly afterwards.

"Police," O'Reilly said. "Graham Quinn?"

"That's me. What do you want?"

"We need to talk to you about your time spent away at the tax-payer's expense, Mr Quinn."

"That was a long time ago. I paid for what I did and I've kept my nose clean ever since."

"If you don't mind," O'Reilly said. "I'd prefer not to discuss this with a six-by-four-inch speaker."

"You'd better come in then."

The door made a buzzing sound and DC Stone pushed it open.

"After you, sir," he said to O'Reilly.

Graham Quinn's apartment was much smaller than O'Reilly expected it to be but he soon realised it looked smaller because it was in a state of utter disarray. There were clothes scattered all over the three-piece-suite and dirty cups and glasses had been left on the coffee table and sideboard. There was a strange smell inside the apartment – it was the stale odour often found in houses where the windows hadn't been opened for quite some time. Quinn was a strange-looking man. He was very tall and his neck was unusually long. When he leaned down to look at O'Reilly, he resembled a giraffe crouching to get something to drink.

"You'll have to excuse the mess," Quinn said. "The cleaning woman only comes on a Tuesday. I can't afford to have her twice a week anymore."

He grinned at O'Reilly and the Irish detective wasn't sure if he was being serious or not.

Quinn shifted some clothes off the two-seater. "Take a seat. What's this all about – I told you, I did my time."

O'Reilly inspected the two-seater and decided it was safe to sit down. "Why exactly did you go to jail?"

Jim Peters had mentioned something about breaking and entering but he hadn't elaborated.

"It was minor stuff," Quinn said. "Me and a mate got a bit drunk one night and broke into a house up in L'Ancresse. We got caught by the security guard there. All we nicked was a couple of laptops and some jewellery."

"And you were sent to jail for that?" DC Stone said.

"My mate got off with a slap on the wrists," Quinn said. "But I was on my last warning – I had form, so they sent me to up to St Sampson's for a few months. It wasn't so bad. Why are you so interested in that all of a sudden?"

"Do you know a man by the name of Steven Banner?" O'Reilly changed tack.

The change in Graham Quinn's facial expression was a subtle one, but O'Reilly noticed it.

"Can't say I know anyone by that name," Quinn said.

"What about James Locke?" DC Stone asked.

"Nope. I'm afraid I can't help you."

"That's a damn shame," O'Reilly said. "I hate it when this happens. It tends to make me irritable."

"What are you talking about? When what happens?"

"When people lie to me. It really gets my goat. Perhaps you ought to have a bit of a think. Perhaps something will come to you when you're not under so much pressure to remember." He took out one of his cards and handed it to Quinn. "Give me a ring if something does come to you. Steven Banner and James Locke. We won't take up anymore of your time. I can see you're busy right now. Washing day, is it?"

50

Graham Quinn didn't reply.

"Come on," O'Reilly said to DC Stone. "We're wasting our time here."

He walked out of the room without saying anything further. DC Stone stood up and followed him out.

CHAPTER ELEVEN

"I don't get it, sir," DC Stone said when they'd got back inside the car. "We've got Quinn's prints from the latest container to be hit. Why didn't we just arrest him?"

"I don't just want Quinn, Andy," O'Reilly turned the key in the ignition. "I want all of them. I want the ones who carried out the robberies – the people who organised it and the ones who are responsible for moving the stolen goods. Get hold of Katie and inform her I want Banner and Locke watched. Graham Quinn is going to get in touch with them, you mark my words. One of them is going to lead us straight to the loot."

As they drove away from Graham Quinn's apartment O'Reilly spotted something in his rear-view mirror that caused him to press his foot down harder on the accelerator. It was a black Toyota Yaris and it was following closely behind. O'Reilly increased his speed but the car behind did the same.

"Andy," he said. "I'm going to do something I've never done before. I'm going to brake-check that bastard who's following us."

DC Stone turned around to see what O'Reilly was talking about. "How do you know they're following us?"

"Because I was followed earlier by exactly the same car. Katie will confirm it."

"You can't see through the windows. They're tinted."

"We'll see who they are when they have no option but to slam into the back of me."

"Do you think that's such a good idea, sir?"

"It's a terrible idea," O'Reilly said. "But I'm not going to let them drive away again. Brace yourself."

O'Reilly watched the black Yaris in his mirror. It didn't appear to be following so closely behind now. But then it accelerated and came within metres of O'Reilly's rear bumper.

"Let's see how you like this."

"I don't think you should..."

DC Stone's sentence was cut short as O'Reilly slammed his foot down on the brakes. Both men lurched forwards and shortly afterwards they were jerked towards the windscreen as the Black Toyota slammed into the back of them.

"Shit," DC Stone said.

"Are you alright?" O'Reilly asked him.

He nodded. "I think so."

"Get out. I'm going to see who's been following me."

He opened the door and peered out at the car behind him. The two airbags in the front were preventing him from seeing who was in the black Yaris.

"Be careful," he warned DC Stone.

They approached the black car and O'Reilly jumped when the passenger door was flung opened. He braced himself for an attack. If this was Patrick Finney, he knew things were about to get ugly. He also knew he ought to call it in. Finney was a wanted man and an extremely dangerous one at that.

The dazed-looking young man who got out of the Toyota wasn't Patrick Finney. This man looked to be at least half the age of Ireland's most notorious serial killer. An older man emerged from the passenger side.

"What the hell were you playing at?" he asked.

"What was I playing at?" O'Reilly said. "Your man there got so close to my arse I was worried we were about to enter into some kind of relationship. Where did you learn to drive, lad?"

On closer inspection O'Reilly realised the driver wasn't long out of school. He was tall and lanky and he still had the evidence of acne on his chin and forehead.

"I'm sorry," he managed.

"He's only just passed his test," the older man said. "He's legal to drive, but I insisted I give him a few more lessons before I let him loose on his own. I'm his dad. What are you going to do about the damage to his car?"

O'Reilly thought hard. He remembered when he passed his driving test. It was a momentous occasion in his life – suddenly the freedom of the open road was his for the taking and he really didn't want to ruin that for this young man.

He looked at the damage to the cars. The Yaris appeared to have come out worst. The front bumper was hanging off and the number plate was lying on the road beneath it. His old car seemed to have come out virtually unscathed.

"I'm sure you're aware," he said. "That in the eyes of the law this is going to come across as your boy's fault. He rammed into the back of me, and whether I slammed on brakes or not is irrelevant, he was driving far too closely behind me. As far as I can see the damage to your son's car is fixable, and I'm sure you'll agree it'll be best not to get the insurance companies involved."

"You don't want to know how much I pay," the driver's father said.

"I can imagine, and a prang like this is going to hit your premiums hard."

"Not to mention the excess," DC Stone added.

Twenty minutes later O'Reilly engaged first gear and eased his foot off the clutch. The car pulled away from the side of the road and DC Stone let out an audible sigh.

"Are you going to tell me what that was all about?" he asked.

"I'm probably being a bit paranoid," O'Reilly said. "Sorry about that."

"Why would you think someone was following you?"

"I've got a suspicious nature, that's all."

O'Reilly didn't feel like elaborating. The father of the young driver of the car had agreed they would keep the accident under wraps. He would get the car fixed without involving the Police or the insurance company. His son promised to be more careful in the future.

O'Reilly's phone started to ring. He turned on the hands free.

"Sir," it was DC Owen. "Steven Banner and James Locke had a visitor and now they're on the move."

"That was quick," O'Reilly said. "Let me guess – this visitor looks like he belongs in the African bush with the other giraffes?"

"Who is he?"

"Graham Quinn. I had a feeling he would get hold of Banner and Locke."

"They're getting into a white van. Do you want me to follow them?"

"Keep your distance," O'Reilly said. "And don't let them know you're there."

"I can do stealth."

"Keep your phone on. I want to know where you are the whole time."

Half an hour later DC Owen informed O'Reilly the white van had come to a stop in St Martin.

"They're getting out, sir," she said.

"Where exactly are you?" O'Reilly asked.

"It's an apartment complex. Les Paradis. It's one of the fancy ones looking out over Saint's Bay."

"I know it," DC Stone said. "We're about two minutes away."

"Stay in the car," O'Reilly said. "I'll organise some back-up."

"What do you think they're doing here?" DC Owen said.

"Getting rid of the stolen goods if I'm not mistaken."

Les Paradis wasn't a large complex. The whole estate was surrounded by a palisade fence that had been painted green. O'Reilly stopped next to DC

Owen's car and he and DC Stone got out. The white van could be seen just inside the gate.

DC Owen came over to O'Reilly.

"Do we know who lives here?" he asked her.

"I spoke to the security guard," she said. "And according to him the apartment the van's parked outside belongs to Mr and Mrs Harris."

"Bernard Harris?" O'Reilly said. "So, he was lying to us – he told us he was single. I wonder what else he's lied to us about."

Another car pulled up alongside them and DCI Fish and DS Skinner got out.

"What have we got?" Fish asked.

"I'm not quite sure yet," O'Reilly told him. "Andy and I paid Graham Quinn a visit and straight after he went to see Steven Banner and James Locke. Katie followed them here. I've got a feeling in my gut they're up to something."

"Let's go and see then," DCI Fish said.

CHAPTER TWELVE

The security guard manning the gate at the Les Paradis apartment complex let them inside and promised not to let anybody leave. It turned out he was a retired police sergeant and he missed the thrill of the chase.

O'Reilly and DCI Fish went in first. The DCs Owen and Stone went in behind them and DS Skinner waited by the gate with the security guard.

"Bernard Harris is behind all of this," O'Reilly said to DCI Fish. "I knew there was something not right about the man."

"Something doesn't add up," DCI Fish said. "He's in charge down at the container depot – surely he would know we'd suspect him."

"Perhaps his arrogance is stronger than his common sense. Shall we ring the bell, or do you think it would be better to barge in unannounced?"

"We'll do this properly, Liam."

DCI Fish rang the bell and soon afterwards the door was opened by a young woman. She was tall and slim and her mousy blond hair was tied back in a tight ponytail.

She looked at O'Reilly and smiled. "Can I help you?"

"Mrs Harris?" O'Reilly asked.

"That's right."

"Island Police," DCI Fish said. "Can we come inside?"

There was a loud crash inside the apartment followed by the sound of raised voices. O'Reilly didn't wait to be invited in. He pushed past Mrs Harris and ran down the hallway. DCI Fish followed behind him.

Steven Banner and James Locke were in the living room. Steven was very red in the face and when O'Reilly looked more closely, he could see he had a swollen lip and a bloody nose.

"Sorry to interrupt," O'Reilly said. "Having a bit of an argument, are you?"

"What do you want now?" Locke asked. "This is police harassment."

"Where's your friend Graham?" O'Reilly said.
The sound from the next room answered his question. O'Reilly nodded to Steven Banner and left the room.

He wasn't quite prepared for what he found. Graham Quinn was shifting boxes around in what appeared to be some kind of sitting room. The boxes were stacked up almost to the ceiling and when he read the labels on them O'Reilly realised the boxes were full of mobile phones and electrical equipment.

He looked at Graham Quinn. "I'd say you lot are pretty buggered, wouldn't you, Graham?"
"I don't know anything about this stuff," Graham said.
"We'll discuss that somewhere more appropriate," DCI Fish said.
"I'll get hold of DI Peters," O'Reilly said. "Jim is going to have his work cut out with this one."

* * *

Steven Banner was the one who told them everything. O'Reilly was shocked at what he heard. It wasn't what he'd been expecting to hear at all. Bernard Harris' wife Sonja was the one who had come up with the idea. Sonja persuaded Bernard to join forces with Graham Quinn, Steven Banner and James Locke. The sixth member of the team was a man by the name of Harry Lincoln. The plan was simple and Sonja believed it was ingenious. Bernard would wait until a container worth hitting came in – he would contact Graham and Harry and tell them which container to break into and when to do so. The security at the container terminal wasn't great and Bernard knew when exactly to send the two men in.

Steven and James' dismissal from the terminal was a slight hitch, as Sonja knew the Police would come calling on them, but she countered this by suggesting they leave the island while three of the robberies were due to take place thus giving them perfect alibis. Steven and James were responsible for offloading the goods. James had a number of contacts and the merchandise was easily converted into cash.

Sonja deduced there was no way the Police would be able to connect her and Bernard to Steven, James, Graham and Harry, and she'd planned two more robberies for the middle of next week.

When O'Reilly and DC Stone paid Graham Quinn a visit, the giraffe-necked ex-con had become rattled and headed over to Steven and James' apartment straight away. James had suggested they take the van to Bernard's apartment and get rid of the stolen goods before the Police put two and two together but they hadn't counted on O'Reilly acting so quickly.

Harry Lincoln hadn't yet been apprehended but O'Reilly was confident he would be found before the end of the day. All in all, it had been an eventful day and one O'Reilly wanted to forget all about.

"That was some great work, Liam," Superintendent Hayes said. O'Reilly sat opposite her in her office.

"It was a great piece of teamwork," he said. "I've got a good team behind me."

"How did you know Bernard Harris' wife was involved?"

"I didn't," O'Reilly admitted. "I didn't even know he was married – he told us he was single and I didn't think to doubt him. I knew Steven Banner and James Locke had some part in it and I thought the same thing about Graham Quinn, so I just kept a keen eye on them. I was lucky."

"The luck of the Irish?"

"That's a myth, Ma'am. The Irish are no luckier than anyone else."

"It was outstanding detective work, nevertheless."

"We still haven't picked up the sixth member of the gang," O'Reilly said. "I've put the word out but Harry Lincoln seems keen to stay hidden."

"He'll turn up. Bad pennies always do in the end."

"I'll let you get on then. I'm just glad we got there in the end."

O'Reilly turned the key in the ignition and drove away from the station. The wind had died down to nothing more than a gentle breeze. By the time O'Reilly had driven the short distance to his apartment he realised he must have checked his rear-view mirror over a dozen times to see if anyone was following him. Nobody was and he wondered if he was being overly-cautious. If Patrick Finney was on the island and out for revenge, he would show his face soon enough and O'Reilly knew there was nothing he could do to stop that from happening. All he could do was wait and hope he was prepared. DC Owen had mentioned something about a full moon tonight and this only served to heighten the sense of foreboding O'Reilly had felt since the incident with the brick that morning.

He let himself into the apartment and glanced at the window the brick had come hurtling though. The glaziers had been and it looked as though nothing had happened. Bram ambled up to him and O'Reilly bent down and stroked his back.

"Have you figured out the enigma of the cat flap yet, cat?"

The contented purrs coming from the ginger tom told O'Reilly the cat flap was the last thing on Bram's mind.

Assumpta was in the kitchen chopping some onions.

"It looks like the glaziers did a good job," O'Reilly said.

"They were in and out within an hour," Assumpta said. "They weren't cheap, though."

"Who is, these days? What are you cooking?"

"I've invited Andy round. I'm making us a Thai curry."

"I'm going out with Victoria," O'Reilly reminded her.

"That's why I invited Andy round."

"Grand. It's bad enough I have to look at his repulsive face all day – I don't think I can face it after hours. It's enough to put a man off his food."

"You're terrible. You will grow to like him one day."

"I very much doubt that," O'Reilly took a beer from the fridge, opened the cap and took a long swig. "I'm going to grab a shower. It's been a very long day. Looks like we nabbed the container robbers."

"That's grand," Assumpta said. "I want to know details."

"Before Fred the Ed gets wind of it, you mean?"

"I like to stay one step ahead of the Herald."

"All in good time. It's still early days. There's still a heap of details to sift through but I promise you, you'll be the first to know. Now, I'm going to have a shower, wash the day away and I'm going to think of nothing else but dinner with the most beautiful woman on this island."

"Thanks, Dad."

"Sorry," O'Reilly said. "I meant the second most beautiful woman on the island."

He came back in the kitchen fifteen minutes later. The smell of the Thai curry was making his mouth water.

"That smells delicious. You're spoiling that rodent."

"Dad," Assumpta said. "Stop calling him that."

"Well, I'll leave you to it. I wouldn't want to keep Victoria waiting."

"Did you lock the door when you went out earlier?" Assumpta said out of the blue.

"What?" O'Reilly said.

"When I got home from work the front door was unlocked."

"I always lock the door. Are you sure you didn't forget to lock it?"

"You locked up, remember. You insisted on driving me to work and I got in the car before you. You were the last one out."

"I can't remember not locking the door," O'Reilly said. "But I suppose it can happen. I'll try to be more careful in the future."

"I got the feeling someone had been here when I got home too," Assumpta turned off the gas hob.

"What do you mean?"

"Just a feeling that someone had been inside. It's hard to explain. It was like the air was different somehow. Like the molecules had shifted because someone new had been here. I'm probably just being paranoid."

"Probably," O'Reilly didn't believe this for a second.

Assumpta's sixth sense was rarely wrong and if she sensed someone had been inside the apartment it probably meant they had.

"Nothing's been taken, has it?" he asked.

"Not as far as I can see. It was probably Bram letting air in from the cat flap."

"I'll remember to lock the door in future," O'Reilly said. "I'll see you later."

CHAPTER THIRTEEN

Victoria Radcliffe was already there when O'Reilly walked through the doors of the Red Snapper. O'Reilly checked his watch and realised he was ten minutes late. He walked over to the table she was sitting at.

"Sorry I'm late. I didn't realise how long I'd spent in the shower."

She smiled at him. "I thought you looked slightly more shrivelled than usual."

"Thanks," O'Reilly kissed her on the cheek and sat down opposite her.

"I've only just got here myself," Victoria said. "I've ordered us a couple of pints."

"You're a woman after my own heart. How are things?"

"Quietening down a bit. The end of September is a strange time for the shop – it can be either busy as anything or absolutely dead. What about you?"

"It's been a tiring day. We got a bit of luck and managed to nab the scumbags who were hitting the containers."

"The luck of the Irish?"

"Something like that. Anyway, I'm not here to talk about that. I'm here to enjoy the company of the most beautiful woman on the island of Guernsey."

Victoria laughed. "Don't let Assumpta hear you say that."

"She's not here to hear me. What do you feel like eating?"

"Something from the sea."

"Good idea."

The drinks arrived and O'Reilly and Victoria both ordered the calamari. The waiter assured them the new chef knew how to cook it perfectly.

"I just hope it's not rubbery," O'Reilly said.

He remembered ordering calamari a while back and he remembered not being able to eat it. It was like chewing through a pile of rubber bands.

"Tommy has suggested we close the shop for a week early next month," Victoria said. "Kawasaki Head Office have given their approval and it'll do Tommy and I good to just get away from bikes for a bit. I was thinking about a holiday."

"That's grand," O'Reilly drained what was left in his glass. "Where are you thinking of going?"

"I was thinking of both of us going away, Liam."

"A holiday?"

"Somewhere a bit warmer than the island. The Canary Islands perhaps – it's still nice and warm there in early October. What do you think?"

"A holiday?" O'Reilly said once more.

"It's where people go away somewhere and leave their lives behind for a bit."

"I know what a holiday is," O'Reilly said.

This wasn't strictly true. In fact, O'Reilly couldn't remember the last time he'd been away on holiday. During his final few years in the Gardai he'd probably only managed to get away for a few days at a time. That was one of the reasons he came to the island in the first place. The long hours and the stress of always being at work was starting to take its toll.

"I'm not sure I'll be able to get the time off," he said. "I've only been in the job five minutes."

"You've been here more than six months," Victoria corrected. "I'm sure you'll have some holiday owed to you."

"I'll check. I've never been to the Canary Islands."

"Me neither, but they sound lovely."

The food arrived and O'Reilly was glad the calamari was cooked properly. He finished first.

"You were hungry," Victoria put down her knife and fork. "I think that's the first time you've beaten me."

"That was delicious," O'Reilly said. "Do you think they do calamari in the Canary Islands?"

"I'm sure they do. So, it's settled then?"

"I'll still have to speak to Personnel," O'Reilly said. "But if I can get a week off, I'm all yours."

She leaned over the table and kissed him on the lips. "It'll be wonderful. We can take walks on the beach, and maybe hire a car and go where not many people go. It'll be just what the doctor ordered."

O'Reilly was about to say something further when his thoughts were interrupted by the sound of someone coughing. It was very loud and the person wheezing and spluttering didn't sound healthy at all. He turned around to see who it was. A haggard woman had come inside the restaurant and parked herself on the table next to the window. O'Reilly turned back around. He didn't want the woman to see him – it was the same woman who'd been arguing with DS Skinner by the front desk that morning. Mrs O'Connell. O'Reilly still couldn't remember where he'd met her before.

He turned his attention back to Victoria. "The night's still young – do you want something else to drink?"

"I don't have to be up early tomorrow," she replied. "So, I'm all yours."

"Glad to hear it. I need to go to the Gents – I'll get us a couple more pints on the way back."

Mrs O'Connell was still coughing. It was so loud O'Reilly could hear it inside the toilets. She didn't sound well. The coughing stopped when he approached the bar to order the drinks.

"Shall I stick it on your bill?" the barman asked.

"Thanks," O'Reilly said.

He picked up the drinks and when he turned around, he found himself face to face with Mrs O'Connell. The reek of her made him take a step back.

She stank of alcohol and something even worse. It was the unmistakable stench of decay and death.

"Hello, Smiley," she said.

O'Reilly winced. The fetid waft of air that came from her mouth made him gag.

"You're a bastard," she added. "Gardai bastard."

O'Reilly ignored her. He walked past her back to his table.

"Do you know that strange woman?" Victoria asked him.

"She looks familiar, but I can't quite place where I know her from. She's got a Dublin accent and she seems to know me so I've probably arrested her at some time or other."

"She doesn't look very well."

"Her body has been addled by all the booze she's had over the years. Hopefully she'll clear off soon. Let's talk about that holiday."

Victoria's phone started to ring in her handbag. She took it out and frowned at the screen.

"It's Tommy."

"Answer it," O'Reilly said.

"It's probably not urgent."

"There's only one way to find out. Answer it."

"Tommy," Victoria said. "I'm over in the capital."

O'Reilly watched her facial expression turn from slight annoyance to what he could only think was shock. Her eyes grew large and her mouth opened wider.

"I'll be there as soon as I can," she said and rang off.

"Problems?" O'Reilly said.

"I don't know," Victoria said. "Tommy got a call from someone telling him the alarm was going off at the shop. When he got there, he realised someone had broken in."

"Good God. Let's go."
"The Police are already there, Liam," Victoria told him. "Tommy phoned them as soon as he realised what had happened."
"Does he know if they took much?"
"He's not sure yet. I have to get over there."
"I'll come with you," O'Reilly offered.
"There's no need for that. Like I said, the Police are already there and there's not much you'll be able to do. I'll give you a ring when I get there."
She stood up and took out her purse.
"Put that away," O'Reilly said. "This is my side of the island, remember. I'm paying."
He stood up and hugged her. "Let me know if there's anything I can do."

CHAPTER FOURTEEN

O'Reilly decided to order another beer. He didn't feel like going home and having to endure the dubious pleasure of DC Stone's company. He looked around the restaurant. The Red Snapper was quiet. It was Monday evening and the tourist season was drawing to a close. There were a few people he recognised at the bar. One of those was DC Owen's father, Tony. Tony was forced into early retirement from the Police due to a heart condition. O'Reilly was the one who had replaced him as DI and for a while they hadn't exactly seen eye to eye, but that had all changed and O'Reilly had grown to respect the man. He was straight-talking and loyal, and his daughter was the detective O'Reilly preferred to work with above everybody else. O'Reilly didn't feel like sitting at the table by himself, so he got up and walked over to the bar.

"Tony," he said. "It's been a while."

"Liam," the ex-DI said. "I've been a bit preoccupied with home improvements. Mrs Owen insisted."

"And you don't argue when they insist," O'Reilly said.

"That you don't. Are you drinking alone?"

"I was with Victoria, but someone broke into the bike shop over in Vazon. The Police are there, so she told me there was no point in me going with her."

"What's happening on this island?" Tony said. "In my day we never used to have these problems. These container robberies never used to happen either."

"It looks like we've wrapped that one up. We had a stroke of luck and that daughter of yours has the intuition of a fox. She's an asset to the team."

"She gets that from her mother," Tony said. "The intuition, I mean. Pint?"

O'Reilly drained his glass. "Might as well, thanks. My beautiful daughter is at home entertaining DC Stone. I can't for the life of me figure out what she sees in the man – I've worked with him for six months and I still haven't come across one redeeming feature."

"There's no accounting for taste. Look at the state of that."

He pointed to the haggard woman from Dublin. Mrs O'Connell was slumped in the chair by the window. Five empty pint glasses stood on the table in front of her.

"She's a lost cause alright," O'Reilly held up his glass. "I know her from somewhere. I think our paths crossed sometime back in Dublin."

"Well, she seems to know you. She's looking this way."

Mrs O'Connell raised a hand in the air and offered them a wave.

"God," O'Reilly said. "She's coming over."

The hollow-eyed woman staggered up to them.

"How about you buy an old friend a drink, Smiley?"

"It looks like you've had enough," O'Reilly said.

"I'm off to the Gents," Tony said and walked away, leaving O'Reilly with his repulsive compatriot.

"Come on, Smiley," she wasn't giving up. "Let's have one for the old country."

"I think it would be best if you left right now."

The stench of her was making him feel sick.

He wasn't expecting what happened next. Mrs O'Connell grabbed hold of his arm and yanked him towards her. She was stronger than O'Reilly expected her to be.

"You think we're scum because you ran away to this island? You think you can leave the old country behind and forget about the likes of me? You can't run from what you are, Smiley. You can't just forget – it doesn't work like that."

She was still holding on to his arm. O'Reilly tried to shrug her off, but her grip was relentless.

"Go home," he said. "Get off me before I do something I might regret."

"We've all got regrets, Smiley. The name's O'Connell. Do you remember now? Delores O'Connell?"

O'Reilly put his hand on hers and yanked it away from his arm. She staggered backwards, and fell flat on her face next to the bar. Their skirmish had now attracted a small audience. A couple sitting a few tables away were looking on with obvious disgust. The barman looked at O'Reilly and the Irish detective shook his head.

DC Owen's dad had returned from the Gents.

"Is everything alright?"

"Mrs O'Connell was just leaving," O'Reilly said.

He held out his hand to her. "Get up. I think it's time you left."

She refused the hand and managed to get on her feet. "Bastard." She looked around the room. "They're all bastards."

She glared at O'Reilly and staggered out of the restaurant.

"The drink has fried her brain," O'Reilly said to Tony.

"What happened?"

"She grabbed hold of me and when I tried to get her off, she fell down. She's rat-arsed."

"You say you don't know who she is?"

"Her face rings a bell, but I can't picture where I've seen her before."

"You knew her name though."

"She told me her name just before you came back from the Gents," O'Reilly said. "I really can't remember where I know her from."

Tony nodded. "I suppose you're right. The longer we spend in the job the more the faces of the scumbags we've arrested fade into the background."

"I'll get another round in."

Twenty-minutes later Tony finished what was left in his glass.
"Time for me to hit the road. I've got a load of kitchen shelves to put up tomorrow and I don't want to do that with a thick head. It was good to see you again."
"You too," O'Reilly said. "I suppose I'd better be off myself. Hopefully the scabby rat in my daughter's life will have gone home already."
"You can't pick who they fall for."
Tony picked up his coat, nodded to O'Reilly and walked away from the bar.

O'Reilly paid his bill and finished what was left in his glass. He said goodbye to the barman and walked past the couple who'd witnessed the incident with Mrs O'Connell. The man looked away, but the woman glared at him as he walked past. O'Reilly shrugged it off. He really couldn't give a damn what people thought of him anymore.

The wind had picked up once more when O'Reilly got outside. It was a chilly wind and it crept inside O'Reilly's coat as he walked. He couldn't wait to get home to the warmth of his apartment. The sky was clear and the full moon lit up the path beautifully. O'Reilly turned the corner and for a brief moment the high buildings offered some respite from the howling wind. He spotted something up ahead. There was something on the pavement in front of the Butchers shop around the corner from his apartment. The light of the moon was reflecting off something shiny. O'Reilly walked up to it and the stench hit his nostrils straight away. It was the reek of stale alcohol and unwashed clothes but mixed in with it now was something else – something all too familiar. It was the metallic tang of fresh blood. It was blood that had been shed very recently.

O'Reilly bent down and winced as the stench became stronger. The moonlight was making it quite clear what he was looking at. Delores O'Connell had offered her final word of abuse. The haggard woman from Dublin was drenched in blood from her throat to her stomach. O'Reilly put his hand over his mouth and fought back the urge to gag. As he did so he felt a hand on his back and he fell forwards. Something exploded inside his head and he collapsed on top of the dead woman outside the Butchers.

CHAPTER FIFTEEN

It was the vile reek that woke O'Reilly a short time later. It felt like he was drowning in it. The stench was in the back of his throat and the inside of his nose. His head was throbbing and for a moment he had no idea where he was. He sat up and felt the wind in his face. Delores O'Connell's face was now lit up in the glare of the moon. Her eyes were open and O'Reilly had to look away. There was something in her gaze that he'd seen too many times before – it was an expression of pure terror. He realised he was holding something in his hand. He looked down and gasped when he saw what it was. He released his grip on the knife and threw it against the door of the Butchers.

He got to his feet and tried to process everything in his mind. None of this made any sense. He remembered leaving the Red Snapper and he remembered the icy wind, but after that, things became a bit hazy. What had happened to Delores O'Connell and how did he end up lying on top of her?

The sound of voices distracted him from his thoughts. They were the voices of a man and a woman, and they were getting closer. O'Reilly didn't know what to do. His detective brain was telling him he knew exactly what he needed to do but his instincts were telling him something else altogether. The man and woman were even closer now. They rounded the corner and started walking straight towards him. As they got closer O'Reilly could see it was the couple who'd been in the Red Snapper earlier.

It was the woman who spotted him first. Her eyes fell on his face, she stopped in her tracks then her gaze was lowered and she focused on the dead woman on the ground. Her mouth started to open and then she screamed.

O'Reilly held up his hands. "It's alright, I'm a detective with the Island Police."

She didn't seem to hear him. Her gaze alternated between him and Delores O'Connell.

Her screaming stopped and the man she was with stepped forwards. "What's going on?"

"I don't know," O'Reilly said. "I found her like this."

"Call the Police," the woman said.

"I *am* the Police," O'Reilly reminded her.

"What have you done?" the woman said and backed off a few paces.

"I found her like this," O'Reilly said. "I'm going to phone it in."

"You killed her," the woman clearly wasn't listening to him. "You killed her."

The throbbing in O'Reilly's head was getting worse. "You need to calm down. I'm going to phone the Police and they'll sort it out when they get here."

"You killed her," the woman said again, much quieter this time.

She reached out for the man's arm but he was too far away and she only managed to find a piece of his shirt. She slid down his body and collapsed onto the ground.

Ten minutes later the area around the Butchers was a hive of activity. Two Police cars had arrived on the scene first followed soon afterwards by an ambulance. DCI Tom Fish had turned up a few minutes later and now he and DS Skinner were speaking to O'Reilly across the road.

"Talk to me, Liam," DCI Fish said. "What's going on?"

"I don't know what's going on, Tom," O'Reilly said. "My head is spinning and I can't think straight. I was out for a meal with Victoria – she was called away so I stayed and had a few drinks with Tony Owen. The dead woman was in the restaurant – her name's Delores O'Connell."

"You know her, then?" DS Skinner asked.

"Her face rings a bell," O'Reilly said. "But I can't place where I've seen her before. She was the woman you spoke to earlier. The one who wanted to report a case of sexual abuse. She started harassing me by the bar."
"Harassing you, how?" DCI Fish said.
"She grabbed hold of me. I told her to stop and when she didn't, I pushed her away from me and she fell. She left right after that, I stayed for another drink then set off home. I found her on the way."

DCI Fish scratched his nose. "The man in the ambulance with his wife said they found you next to the victim looking dazed. And you've got blood all over your jacket."
"I don't know what happened," O'Reilly said. "I bent over to check to see if she was still alive and I think someone attacked me."
"You think?" It was DS Skinner.
"I told you, I don't know what happened. One minute I was leaning over her then I woke up on top of her with a knife in my hand and a throbbing headache."
"A knife?" This was clearly news to DCI Fish.
"I don't know how it got there. I threw it on the ground. I really don't know what happened."

"Are you alright now?" DCI Fish asked. "Do you need medical attention?"
"I'll be fine. I have a throbbing headache and things are a bit of a blur but I have no idea what happened here."
"And you definitely don't know the victim?"
"I told you, her face rings a bell. She was by the front desk when I came to work this morning, babbling all sorts of nonsense. She's from Dublin but I have no idea what she's doing on the island."
"This is all very confusing," DCI Fish said. "An Irish woman comes in to report an assault and the same night she's found dead by one of the detectives she spoke to."

The fog inside O'Reilly's head was starting to clear. "I think I might have an idea what this could be all about."

"Go on," DCI Fish urged.

"Patrick Finney. Finney escaped from prison and I think he's on the island."

"What has that got to do with what happened to Mrs O'Connell?" DS Skinner asked.

"Things have been happening and I think Finney is behind it."

"I'm still not following you, Liam," DCI Fish said.

"I think he's come here for revenge. I was the one who put him away. That was fifteen years ago, and I think he's come here to get his revenge."

"Where does Mrs O'Connell come into the equation?"

"I was the one who found her. One minute I'm leaning over her body and the next I'm waking up on top of her with a knife in my hand."

"What are you saying?" DS Skinner said. "This Finney character killed Mrs O'Connell so he could frame you for her murder?"

"That's exactly what I'm starting to think," O'Reilly said.

"That sounds a bit far-fetched, Liam," DCI Fish said. "If not pretty impossible. There is no way Finney could know you'd be anywhere near here. How could he know you would be the one to find the body?"

"This was Finney's work," O'Reilly realised he'd raised his voice. "You don't know what this man is capable of. It has him written all over it. There's even a full moon, for feck's sake."

"What has that got to do with anything?" DS Skinner said.

"Finney killed four women," O'Reilly said. "All of them were murdered when the moon was full. He left a calling card at each crime scene. I'm being set up."

"I think it would be best if you got yourself checked out," DCI Fish said. "If you did get bashed on the head, you could have a concussion."

"What do you mean, *if* I got bashed on the head?" O'Reilly could feel his face heating up. "Don't you believe me?"

"All I know is things are very confused at the moment. We'll have a clearer picture of what happened when Forensics is finished, but right now I suggest you either get yourself checked out by the paramedics or go home and get some rest."

"I'm fine," O'Reilly said. "Finney is on this island and this is just the beginning – you mark my words."

"Go home, Liam," DCI Fish said. "We'll take it from here."

"What the hell is that supposed to mean? Are you kicking me off the team?"

"I'm doing no such thing. You've been through quite an ordeal – you're probably in shock and the best thing you can do now is go home."

O'Reilly was about to say something else but he realised it was pointless. He shook his head, turned around and headed home.

CHAPTER SIXTEEN

O'Reilly was glad DC Stone had just left when he went inside the apartment. Assumpta was drying dishes in the kitchen.

"Are you alright?" she asked. "You look terrible."

"I feel terrible."

Assumpta pointed to his jacket. "Is that blood?"

O'Reilly told her what had happened.

"Holy crap," she exclaimed when he was finished. "Are you alright?"

"I'm being set up and it appears none of my colleagues believe me. This is all down to Patrick Finney. He killed that woman and he's trying to make it look like I did it."

"How is that even possible?"

"Don't you start too. It's possible."

"Think about it logically, Dad," Assumpta put down the tea towel. "Let's say Finney did kill that poor woman – how would he know you'd be the one to find her?"

"I don't know, but he made sure I did. I think he's been keeping an eye on me."

"Someone else could have stumbled across her body first," Assumpta pointed out. "There is no way Finney could be sure you were going to be the one to find her. No way."

"He made a way. He planned all of this. I Know Finney and I know what he's capable of. I don't know how he did it, but he did. I'm going to have a shower; I can still smell the stench of that woman on me."

He came downstairs ten minutes later. "That's better. What a night."

Bram walked in, looked up at O'Reilly and headed for the cat flap.

"He's getting used to it," Assumpta said as the ginger tom disappeared through the flap.

"About time. I'm worried, Summi. I'm terrified. I've got a feeling this is just the beginning."

"I still can't see how Finney would be able to set something like this up," Assumpta said. "It just isn't possible."

"The woman was at the station when I arrived this morning. Then she showed up at the Snapper. And now she's dead. She was killed less than an hour after she accosted me at the bar."

"I can't see how all that fits together."

"Think about it, Summi," O'Reilly said. "She grabbed hold of me in the restaurant – I shook her off and she fell to the floor. Then I just happen to stumble across her body. Someone attacked me and when I came to, I was lying on top of her body with what's most likely the murder weapon in my hand. I think Delores O'Connell was in on it."

"Now you're being ridiculous, Dad. You're telling me Finney and this woman concocted a plan to frame you for murder? You're forgetting one thing – the woman is dead. Only a mad woman would agree to a plan like that."

"Or a dying one," O'Reilly thought out loud.

"I think you need some sleep. That bang on the head has confused your brain."

"Finney is behind this. And I'm going to beat him. I did it before and I'm going to do it again."

"I'm off to bed," Assumpta said. "I suggest you do the same."

"I'm going to stay up for a bit. There's too much going around in my head."

"I'll see you in the morning."

O'Reilly made some tea and sat back on the sofa. Bram came in and jumped up next to him.

"What do you think, cat?" O'Reilly said. "You don't think I'm losing my mind, do you?"

The long, drawn-out yawn suggested Bram didn't have an opinion on the matter one way or another.

"Finney did this," O'Reilly carried on regardless. "I just have to figure out how he did it."

His phone started to ring on the table next to him. He looked at the screen and sighed. It was DCI Fish.

"Tom," he answered it. "Have you found something?"

"We found the knife," the DCI replied.

"I told you, I threw it on the ground when I realised what it was."

"We've got a problem, Liam. The woman who was there at the scene has made a statement. And it's quite a damaging one as far as you're concerned."

"What are you talking about?"

"She's put it on record that you attacked the dead woman in the Red Snapper and when she and her husband were walking home, she claims you were standing next to Mrs O'Connell with a wild look in your eyes."

"You can't be serious?" O'Reilly couldn't believe what he was hearing.

"I'm afraid I am. This is deadly serious, Liam."

"I'm knackered, Tom," O'Reilly said. "We'll make a start first thing in the morning. I know Patrick Finney had a hand in this and I'll be damned if I'm not going to catch him. I've done it before."

"I'm afraid it's not as simple as that."

"What are you talking about?"

"I'm just giving you a heads-up. There will be an investigation and we will treat this murder the way we treat every murder, and that means nobody is above the law."

"You're talking about me, aren't you?" O'Reilly picked up his tea but his hands were now shaking so badly he had to put the cup straight back down. "You're implying that I'm a suspect, aren't you?"

"It is what it is, Liam. Like I said, I'm giving you a heads-up. Out of professional courtesy, but you need to prepare yourself for a hell of a day tomorrow."

"Professional courtesy?" O'Reilly repeated. "Fuck you, Tom. Fuck you and your professional courtesy."

After hanging up, O'Reilly took a few deep breaths in quick succession and tried to calm down. It wasn't working. He was furious. He finished his tea and rubbed his eyes. He tried to make some sense out of everything. If Patrick Finney had devised a plan to frame him for murder, he had to admit it was a very clever plan. Shortly before the woman is killed O'Reilly is seen involved in an altercation with her – he's found next to her body and he's covered in her blood. O'Reilly realised his fingerprints will also be on the knife used to kill her. All in all, it was an ingenious plan.

"You're forgetting one thing, Finney," he spoke out loud. "Where's the motive?"

The evidence against him was pretty damning but there was one vital part missing – motive. O'Reilly had no reason for wanting Delores O'Connell dead and this offered him a glimmer of hope. Framing someone for murder was trickier than most people realised. You can orchestrate opportunity and fabricate evidence to put someone in the picture, but motive is much harder to concoct. O'Reilly had no reason to kill Delores and surely that in itself should be enough to cast some doubt in the minds of his colleagues.

"Your plan has a hole in it, Finney," he said. "Let's see you dig your way out of that one."

He gave Bram a gentle stroke and headed off to bed.

CHAPTER SEVENTEEN

O'Reilly was still half-asleep when Assumpta knocked on his bedroom door and stood by the bed with a grave expression on her face.

"What time is it?" O'Reilly asked her.

"Just gone seven," she said. "The Police are here."

"The Police?"

"Two PCs. I think they're here to arrest you."

O'Reilly was wide awake now. "Let's see about that, shall we?"

DCI Fish's parting comment about professional courtesy was still fresh in O'Reilly's mind and the two uniformed officers sitting in O'Reilly's living room had clearly been given instructions along those lines. PC Greg Hill and PC Kim London looked more nervous than the man they'd come to see.

"Sorry about this, sir," PC Hill said. "But we have to ask you to come with us."

"I see," O'Reilly said. "Are you arresting me?"

"No, sir," PC London replied. "We were instructed to bring you in for questioning. I'm really sorry about this."

"It's not your fault," O'Reilly assured her.

He wondered why someone in his team hadn't been given the honours.

"Would it be too much to ask for ten minutes to splash some water on my face and grab a cup of tea?" he asked. "I find I can't start the day without a cup of tea in my belly."

"Of course, sir," PC London said.

Bram came in, glared at PC London and turned to face O'Reilly.

"You're in his spot," the Irish detective explained. "He gets quite territorial sometimes."

The young PC shifted to the other side of the couch, Bram jumped up and settled down in his usual place and was soon fast asleep.

"Cats," O'Reilly said. "They're like women – they can't be trained. I'll just have a quick wash and grab a cup of tea."

Twenty minutes later he found himself in the back of a Police car. Assumpta had offered to go with him – O'Reilly had told her it wasn't necessary and he'd also declined her offer of arranging for a solicitor to meet him at the station.

"It's a stupid mistake," he'd said. "A really stupid mistake."

Even though he'd half expected this, he still found it all very hard to digest. Yesterday he was busy wrapping up an investigation that he'd been working on for weeks and now, here he was in the back of a Police car. He was on the other side of the law now.

He was still convinced Patrick Finney was behind his predicament but he needed to prove it, and as things stood, he was in danger of being in no position to obtain that proof. He knew there was a strong possibility of being held in custody for up to three days while the team investigated the murder in his absence. There were more than enough grounds to hold him while they dug deeper, but he hoped and prayed the evidence alone wouldn't be enough for Tom Fish to go that route. He hoped the DCI would give him the benefit of the doubt and offer him some of the professional courtesy he'd spoken of on the phone.

As they drove through the gates towards the car park at the station O'Reilly was relieved that the press hadn't got wind of what had happened yet. He wasn't naïve enough to believe the story wouldn't get out soon enough but the absence of the press right now was something at least.

PC Hill opened the back door and O'Reilly got out.

"I really am sorry about this, sir," he said.

"Stop saying that," O'Reilly said. "I'll soon sort this mess out."

"We were told to take you straight through to one of the interview rooms," PC London informed him.

"I know the way," O'Reilly said. "Don't worry – I'm not going to do a runner."

The two PCs followed close behind him as he made his way down the corridor towards the interview rooms. There was nobody around and O'Reilly wondered if they had picked him up so early for exactly this reason. The rest of his team wouldn't be in yet, and the more he thought about it the more he became convinced this early morning surprise was intentional.

"Would you like something to drink, sir?" PC London asked him.

"A cup of tea would be grand," O'Reilly replied. "There's some in my office. Do you know who will be conducting the interview?"

She shook her head. "We were just told you go and pick you up. I'll fetch you that tea."

PC Hill remained in the interview room with O'Reilly. He looked like he was the one about to be questioned about the recent murder. He was shifting from one foot to the other and his eyes were darting all over the room.

"Get a grip, lad," O'Reilly told him. "You're making me feel giddy."

"Sorry, sir," PC Hill said.

"And stop saying that."

PC London returned with the tea then she and PC Hill left the room. The door opened a short time later and DCO Callum Dove came in and sat down opposite O'Reilly.

The Irish detective was now extremely concerned. "What's going on, sir?"

"How are you feeling, Liam?" Dove asked.

The Deputy Chief Officer's face gave nothing away.

"How am I feeling?" O'Reilly repeated. "I'm feeling like I've been abandoned by the people I work with. That's how I'm feeling. The men and women I work day and night with seem to have turned their backs on me."

"I'm sorry you feel like that," Dove said.

"With respect, sir," O'Reilly said. "What exactly are you doing here? Surely you're not going to be conducting the interview?"

"No," Dove said. "No, I'm not. I'm here in my capacity as DCO. Unfortunately, the Chief Officer couldn't be here himself. CO Johnson is in London until the weekend. I'm here out of professional courtesy."

Those words again, O'Reilly thought.

Those two words were really starting to get on his nerves.

"These are extraordinary circumstances, Liam," DCO Dove continued. "And protocol dictates the manner in which this investigation is to be handled. Obviously, we would prefer to handle this internally but I'm afraid that's not possible in this instance. As I said extraordinary circumstances call for extraordinary measures."

"I'm not following you, sir," O'Reilly said. "A woman was murdered – surely protocol dictates we investigate the same way as always."

"Absolutely not. Firstly, there is no *we* as far as you're concerned, and, secondly in matters such as these there is conflict of interest to take into account."

"I understand I can't be involved in a case when I'm considered a suspect in that case but I don't see where conflict of interest comes into it."

"It's simple, Liam," DCO Dove explained. "Your team will not be involved in this one – they're too close to you and as such it is believed there will be an inevitable clouding of judgment."

O'Reilly took a deep breath and tried to think rationally. He knew the DCO was right – when someone on an investigative team was suspected of a crime it was unprofessional for that team to remain involved in the investigation, but he wished the DCO would offer him the courtesy of the benefit of the doubt.

"I didn't kill that woman, sir," he said.

DCO Dove looked him in the eyes. "Off the record, I believe you."

"Off the record?"

"My position dictates I don't form opinions. That's just how it is."

"OK," O'Reilly said. "What happens next? Who will be conducting the investigation? The last time I looked, there was only one team of detectives in Island HQ and that's the team I used to be part of."

"You are still part of that team, Liam," DCO Dove said. "And I sincerely hope this is all a big misunderstanding and that it will blow over soon. Under the circumstances I've decided the investigation will be shifted into the hands of the Border Agency."

"You can't be serious?"

"Who better to handle it? They have an experienced team and they are more than capable of bringing this matter to its rightful conclusion."

O'Reilly didn't doubt that for a moment. He knew the detectives in the specialist Border Agency were highly experienced officers, but there was one problem with them taking over the investigation. The senior officer in the Border Agency was a man O'Reilly hoped he would never have to go up against again. He and DCI Franklin Urban had clashed heads when O'Reilly first arrived on the island. The Irish detective had made Urban look like a fool and he knew Urban wasn't a man who would easily forget something like that. This situation had just become a whole lot worse.

CHAPTER EIGHTEEN

DCI Franklin Urban was a man used to getting his own way. Driven and ambitious he stopped at nothing in his quest for success. He was arrogant and egotistic and it was these traits that had caused him to stumble when he first became acquainted with O'Reilly. The Irish detective hadn't been on the island a week when Urban had tried to muscle in on an investigation he was working on. When a body was washed up on the shore Urban was convinced the particular brutality inflicted on the victim was the work of Bulgarian drug lords. And as the Border Agency had a number of these drug traffickers under their radar Urban saw fit to insist on taking over the investigation. Ignoring the justifiable protests from O'Reilly he trampled all over O'Reilly and discarded every bit of information he was given.

When it transpired these murders had nothing to do with drug lords Urban was left with so much egg on his face it would be years before anyone forgot the fiasco, and O'Reilly knew a man like him wouldn't forget who was responsible for making him look like an imbecile. His ego had been bruised deeply and it was only a matter of time before he sought an opportunity to settle the score.

So, when DCI Urban came inside the interview room and sat opposite the DI suspected of murder, O'Reilly could see from the smug expression on his face this wasn't going to be plain sailing. DCO Dove's words were still fresh in his head, and if ever there was a conflict of interest within an investigative team now was that time. The arrogant Head of the Border Agency's judgement was likely to be far more clouded than anyone in O'Reilly's team.

"DS Rowland will be along shortly," Urban said. "I trust they've been treating you well since they brought you in?"

"What happened to that woman has nothing to do with the GBA," O'Reilly said.

"Exceptional circumstances call for exceptional courses of action."

O'Reilly could see the arrogant DCI hadn't changed a bit.

"I've had a look through the case notes," Urban continued. "The initial forensic isn't yet complete, but with my team on it that process will be expedited. I have to warn you, Liam it isn't looking good for you. From what I've seen so far, we've got more than enough to charge you, although of course that's the last thing we want to do right now. I assume your legal representation is on the way?"

"No," O'Reilly said. "I haven't requested legal representation."

"That is your right, of course, but I would strongly advise you to reconsider."

"Can we just get on with it? I've got better things to do with my time."

The door opened and a thin man with red hair came in.

"Sorry to keep you waiting," he said and sat down next to Urban.

"This is DS Rowland," Urban said to O'Reilly. "I'm not sure you two have met."

"No," O'Reilly said. "We haven't."

DCI Urban switched on the recording device.

"Interview with Liam O'Reilly started, 08:15. Tuesday, 25th September 2018. Present DI O'Reilly DCI Urban and DS Rowland. For the record DI O'Reilly has declined his right to legal representation. Liam, may I call you Liam for the duration of the interview? It will save confusion if we don't refer to your rank in the Island Police."

"Call me what you want," O'Reilly said.

"OK," Urban said. "Do you know a woman by the name of Delores O'Connell?"

"Her face rang a bell, but I can't be quite sure where I've seen her before. She's from Dublin so our paths might have crossed there at one time."

"In what capacity could your paths have crossed?" It was DS Rowland.

"Mrs O'Connell wasn't what you would describe as a model citizen, that's all. She was a drunk and a vagrant. It's not impossible that I arrested her while I was working in Dublin."

"I see," Urban said. "So, you were acquainted with Mrs O'Connell. Can you talk us through the events yesterday? We have the case notes and we have your version of events according to DCI Fish, but I'd like to hear them from you."

"Where do you want me to start?"

"The beginning is always a good place."

"She was by the front desk when I came to work yesterday," O'Reilly told him. "She was arguing with DS Skinner about not taking an assault report seriously. She told him she couldn't remember when it had happened or who assaulted her, so DS Skinner explained there wasn't much we could do. Then she left, mumbling something about the bastard Gardai."

"That would be the Irish Police?" DS Rowland said.

"Right."

"But that wasn't the last you saw of Mrs O'Connell, was it?" DCI Urban said.

"I went out for a meal with Victoria Radcliffe," O'Reilly said. "To the Red Snapper. She owns the bike shop over in Vazon and she received a phone call to tell her the shop had been broken into and she had to leave. It was still early so I stayed and had a couple of drinks with Tony Owen."

"DI Owen?" DS Rowland said.

"He's retired now," Urban said. "Go on, Liam."

"Mrs O'Connell came inside the restaurant," O'Reilly said. "She spotted me and came over."

"Can Mr Owen corroborate this?"

"Of course. The woman was inebriated and I asked her to leave me alone."

"Did she? Did she leave you alone?"

"No, she didn't. Tony went to the Gents and that's when she grabbed hold of me. I asked her to let go but she didn't."
"Then what happened?"
"I'd had enough so I yanked my arm away from her. She was so drunk she stumbled to the floor and she left soon afterwards."
"Did Mr Owen see this happen?" DS Rowland said.
"It was all over by the time he came back from the Gents."
"Interesting," DCI Urban said.
"What's that supposed to mean?"
"Nothing. And that was the last time you saw her, was it?"
"No," O'Reilly realised he was clenching his teeth. "The last time I saw her was when I realised she was dead outside the Butchers. I didn't kill her – she was already dead when I found her."

"There are a few things I don't quite understand," DCI Urban said. "You told DCI Fish that you woke up on top of her with a knife in your hand?"
"That's exactly what happened?" O'Reilly confirmed.
"How is that possible?"
"I think someone attacked me. I remember crouching over her body, then the next thing I remember I'm lying on top of her with a knife in my hand. Someone attacked me. Someone banged me on the back of the head."
"Did you seek medical attention for this *bang on the head*?" DS Rowland asked.
He said the words, bang on the head with such disdain O'Reilly found himself glaring at the skinny DS.
"No," he said. "I didn't think it was necessary. Tom suggested I go straight home and that's exactly what I did."
"So, there's nothing to confirm you were actually attacked?" DCI Urban said.
"I've just told you I was," O'Reilly said. "And I expect you to believe me."

"Let me get this straight," DCI Urban rubbed his chin. "You were involved in an altercation in a restaurant with a woman and shortly afterwards you discover her dead body? Is that correct?"

"That's exactly what happened."

"And you have no idea how you managed to end up lying on top of her with the murder weapon in your hand?"

"Someone is trying to frame me," O'Reilly came out with it.

"Go on," DCI Urban urged.

"Patrick Finney. He escaped from prison last week and I think he's here on the island. I was the one who put him away fifteen years ago."

"And you believe he's come here to seek revenge?"

"That's exactly what this looks like to me. It was a full moon last night and Finney liked to kill by the light of the full moon. Yesterday morning someone threw a brick through my window with a note attached to it. At the bottom of the note was a crude drawing of Finney's calling card. And later in the day someone phoned my daughter and she was sure it was Finney."

He'd forgotten about the mystery package he'd received.

The room went silent for a moment.

"This is all very well and good, Liam," DCI Urban said. "But there are a few loose ends to your stitch-up theory. If this is as you suspect and Finney is behind it, how would he be so certain you would find the body?"

"I think he's been keeping an eye on me."

"Have you noticed anyone following you?" DS Rowland asked.

"I thought I was being tailed by a black Toyota yesterday, but I didn't see who was driving."

"Nothing else?" DCI Urban said.

"No, but this has Finney written all over it."

"This is how things stand right now," Urban said. "We have a dead woman – we have witnesses who saw you attack her and witnesses who can

put you at the scene of the murder. We have the knife that was used to kill the victim and we'll no doubt find your prints on that knife."
"You will," O'Reilly said. "I told you I woke up with it in my hands."
"And," DS Rowland said. "We have your claim that you were attacked, and that was why you ended up on top of the dead woman, yet you have nothing to corroborate this attack – no witnesses and no evidence of injury."
"That's what happened," O'Reilly said. "That is exactly what happened."

"Do you still have the note?" DCI Urban asked. "The one attached to the brick?"
"I think so."
"You think so?"
"I'm sure it's at home somewhere."
"If it is, we'll find it. We're going to procure a warrant to search your apartment anyway during the course of the day."
"What the hell for?"
"Because this is a murder investigation and that's how things work. I would have thought you would be aware of that. The forensics officers of the GBA will be handling that. You are aware I have more than ample grounds to recommend you remain in custody for the maximum time possible while we investigate further?"
"You've got to be kidding?" O'Reilly could feel his stomach heating up.
"But," DCI Urban continued. "I am not going to do that. I am using my judgment here, and you will be free to go as soon as this interview is over. Don't make me regret this decision. Don't let me down, Liam."

CHAPTER NINETEEN

DCI Urban's words were still burning holes in his ears as O'Reilly walked.
Don't let me down, Liam.
He felt like a schoolchild who'd just been given a dressing down by a teacher.
"Arrogant prick," he said under his breath.

He didn't actually know where he was going. The forensics officers with the GBA were going to conduct a thorough search of his apartment during the course of the day and his presence would be required during that search, but he understood from past experience that procuring a search warrant was a time-consuming process and he didn't feel like pacing up and down at home waiting for the inevitable. He would have gladly let them search his home without the need for a warrant – there was nothing there to incriminate him, but DCI Urban's patronising parting words had made him furious and he decided to make it as difficult as possible for him.

He realised he'd walked half the length of the esplanade without realising it. He sat down on one of the benches and looked out to sea. The wind was picking up again and the sea was choppy. A few daring souls were braving the elements on their yachts some distance out. O'Reilly took out his phone and brought up his daughter's number. He needed to let her know what was happening.
"Summi," he said when the call was answered. "They've let me go but they're going to be searching the apartment."
"What on earth for?" she asked.
"Standard procedure."
"How are you?"

"I've been better. They've taken the case away from my team and my worst nightmare has begun. You'll never guess who they've put in charge of the investigation?"

"Go on."

"Franklin Urban, the Head of the Border Agency."

"Didn't you and he have a falling out when you first came here?"

"You could say that," O'Reilly said. "And I get the feeling he's loving every minute of it. I made him look like a complete prick and now he's been handed a way to get even."

"He can't use his position to do that, Dad."

"Don't be so naïve, Summi," O'Reilly said. "People like Urban relish in opportunities to seek this kind of revenge. He's going to be very disappointed though. When he sees this has nothing to do with me, he'll have no option but to back off."

"I hope you're right. Do you need me to do anything?"

"I'm not sure yet. This is going to get out and when it does, I've got a feeling the press is going to have a field day."

"They're not going to hear anything from me."

"I know. That's not what I'm worried about. A DI suspected of murder will be big news in a place like this, so I need you to be prepared for a bit of backlash."

"I'm a big girl, Dad," Assumpta said. "I'm more worried about you. What time will they be searching the apartment?"

"They'll let me know. Perhaps I should go home now and train Bram how to bite arrogant GBA detectives."

"Good luck with that. It took him long enough to learn how to use a cat flap. I'd better get going. We've got an editorial meeting in a couple of minutes. Phone me if you need me."

"Thanks, Summi. This is probably all going to blow over in a day or two."

He didn't believe that for a second. He stood up and walked back in the direction of the town. The wind was now whipping up eddies of fine sand all along the esplanade and every now and then he had to close his eyes to avoid being stung by the grainy whirlwinds. He wasn't sure what he was going to do. His hands were tied, and he didn't know who to turn to. He couldn't approach anyone on his team – he didn't want any of them to get into trouble on his behalf, and he wasn't exactly sure what any of them would be able to do to help him anyway.

He knew he needed to tell Victoria. The last thing he wanted was for her to hear about it before he'd had a chance to explain what had happened to her. He was sure the gossip mongers on the island would soon start wagging their tongues and when that happened the truth tended to get somewhat distorted. He dialled her number but it went straight to voicemail and he hung up. He hated talking to machines.

His phone started to ring before he'd even put it back in his pocket. He sighed when he saw it was DC Owen's mobile number.

"Katie," he answered it.

"We've just heard, sir," she said. "Superintendent Hayes called us all in and I think it's atrocious. How can they arrest you for murder?"

"I haven't been arrested, Katie," O'Reilly said. "I've been questioned and they're going to search my apartment later, but they didn't arrest me."

"It's still disgusting how they can even harbour the thought of you killing that woman. Is there anything I can do?"

"It would be best if you stayed out of it," O'Reilly said. "The GBA is handling it and it will be best to let them get on with it. They're not going to find anything at my apartment and they'll soon realise I had nothing to do with it."

"We all want to help, sir," DC Owen said. "We were all horrified when we heard how you've been treated. Andy even threatened to go and see Urban to give him a piece of his mind."

This took O'Reilly by surprise. "I appreciate your support, Katie, but this is my problem and I'm not going to drag anyone else into it."

"What are you going to do?"

DC Owen's words had stirred up something inside O'Reilly. Knowing he had to full support of his team had somehow boosted his energy levels and even though he knew he couldn't involve any of them him in this he knew exactly what he had to do.

"I'm going to find Patrick Finney," he said. "If the Police on this island are too blind to see what's happening right now, I'm the only one who's capable of opening their eyes to it."

CHAPTER TWENTY

The call from DCI Urban came three hours later. O'Reilly was eating a light lunch in a café around the corner from the station when his phone started to ring.

"The search is scheduled for half an hour from now." The arrogant Head of the Border Agency didn't offer any small talk. "I would appreciate it if you didn't hold us up."

"I'll be there," O'Reilly told him and rang off.

He paid his bill and headed home. He wanted to get back to the apartment before Urban and his forensic officers arrived. He walked quickly with the wind on his back and turned the key in the lock five minutes later. Bram was nowhere to be seen. The ginger tom had obviously become an expert with the cat flap and was making the most of his new-found freedom.

O'Reilly didn't know why but he started to panic. There was perspiration forming on his forehead and under his arms and he could feel that his heart was beating dangerously fast.

"Calm down," he told himself. "They're not going to find anything."

He wondered exactly what it was they were looking for. As far as he could remember there was nothing here to find. There was nothing inside the apartment that could possibly implicate him in a murder that took place a good distance away. He remembered the note from the brick and began searching for it. He couldn't recall what he'd done with the piece of paper attached to the brick that was thrown through the window.

Had he thrown it away?

He didn't think so. He couldn't recall doing so anyway. He went through to the living room and searched the area around where the brick had landed. The note was nowhere to be seen. He left the room and headed for the kitchen. Perhaps he'd picked up the note and left it there somewhere. He couldn't find it here either.

After a thorough search, O'Reilly sat down at the table and tried to think about where the note could be. He didn't think he would have thrown it in the bin but he set about the unpleasant task of sifting through the rubbish, nevertheless. He took the lid off the bin and the unmistakable stench of cigarette butts hit him. The stale reek was mingled with the smell of old beer. He found the source of the smell in the form of half a dozen beer bottles. At the bottom of most of them were the dog ends of the cigarettes. O'Reilly remembered that DC Stone had been here the night before and realised he must have used the empty bottles as makeshift ashtrays. O'Reilly made a mental note to give the shifty-eyed DC a lecture about this when he got the chance.

Five minutes later he was finished. His hands stank like a pub on a Monday morning – his arms were spattered with leftover curry sauce and he still hadn't found the note that had been attached to the brick.

"Where the hell is it?" he asked himself as he washed his arms and hands in the kitchen sink.

He didn't have time to think about where else he could have put it as the sound of the doorbell told him Franklin Urban and his team had arrived. The Border Agency was about to invade his space and there was nothing he could do about it.

"You know the drill, Liam," DCI Urban didn't wait to be asked inside. He handed O'Reilly a copy of the warrant and the Notice of Rights and Powers then he introduced the officers who would be carrying out the search.

O'Reilly put the documents on the table in the hallway without even bothering to read them. "I would have given my consent if you'd just bothered to ask. You didn't need a warrant?"

DCI Urban's eyes narrowed. "Why didn't you mention this earlier?"

"I believe the onus is on you with that one," O'Reilly said. "You didn't ask."

"Let's get started then. We've already wasted enough time. I need to ask you if you've touched anything."

"Touched anything in my own home?" O'Reilly said. "Of course I have. What sort of a question is that?"

DCI Urban didn't reply to that. "I need you to stay out of our way. You have the right to be present during the search but you will not interfere. Do I make myself clear?"

"Clear as the watered-down beer at the Dublin Student Union, sir," O'Reilly said. "I assume I'm allowed to make myself a cup of tea while I wait?"

"Of course, but do not touch anything else."

"I'll bear that in mind," O'Reilly said and nodded. "You won't mind if I don't offer you and your team a drink though? I wouldn't want to slow things down any further."

"I'll inform you when we're finished."

O'Reilly walked inside the kitchen just as Bram's head appeared from the cat flap. He spotted O'Reilly and rubbed against his legs.

"We've got a bit of a houseful right now, cat," O'Reilly told him. "You'd best stay out of the way."

He filled up Bram's bowl with cat food and turned on the kettle. He could hear the sound of drawers being opened and cupboards being slammed in the next room. DCI Urban's team seemed to be conducting a thorough search.

O'Reilly sat at the table with his tea. Bram had finished his food and gone back outside. The mobile phone on the table started to ring. O'Reilly looked at the screen and saw it was a local number.

"O'Reilly," he answered it.

The line was silent.

"Who is this?" O'Reilly asked.

"How does it feel, Smiley?"

O'Reilly suddenly felt cold. He felt like icy fingers had him by the throat and were hell bent on freezing him from the outside in.

"Are you still there, Smiley?"

The voice hadn't changed much. It was the unmistakable brogue of Dublin but there was a subtle difference now. There was a warmth to the tone that hadn't been there before.

When Patrick Finney was caught, O'Reilly had spent a considerable amount of time with him. Throughout the interviews and the trial Finney's voice had remained cold and unemotional. He'd spoken of his atrocious acts with a coolness that had often chilled O'Reilly to the very core, but his voice sounded different now.

He sounded almost human. There was concern in his voice.

"How does it feel, Smiley," he said again. "It must be quite different to be on the other side for once."

O'Reilly tried to think hard. He needed to act quickly but the fog inside his head had reared its ugly face again. He got up from the table and walked as quietly as possible out of the kitchen and down the hallway. The technicians from the Border Agency were still making quite a din in the living room. The sound of something smashing was followed by a suitable curse from one of Urban's team.

"Sounds like they're wrecking the place, Smiley," Finney said. "How does it feel? To be treated like this?"

"I know you killed Delores O'Connell," O'Reilly said in a voice no more than a whisper.

"I know you know. I'm watching you, remember. Don't you ever forget that. I'll be seeing you, Smiley."

O'Reilly found DCI Urban in the main bedroom. Urban was about to say something but O'Reilly put a finger to his mouth to indicate he needed the DCI to keep quiet.

"I'm going to come for you, Patrick," he spoke into the phone.

"I'll look forward to it, Smiley."

O'Reilly beckoned for Urban to come closer. He repeated his shush signal and handed him the phone. DCI Urban frowned and took the phone.

Patrick Finney.

O'Reilly mouthed the words.

DCI Urban put the phone to his ear and listened. After a short while he shook his head and rolled his eyes.

He handed the phone back to O'Reilly. "There's nobody there, Liam. There was nothing on the other end but the dialling tone."

CHAPTER TWENTY ONE

"It was Finney," O'Reilly said for the third time. "You need to trace the number and find out where he is."

"There was nobody on the line, Liam," DCI Urban said.

"It was him."

"How can you be so sure?"

"Because I spent months listening to the fucking man," O'Reilly said. "I'd know his voice anywhere. It was him. He probably made the call from a phone box but you can still narrow things down a bit. Let me get my team on to it if you can't be bothered."

"Do I have to remind you, you no longer have a team? Until I have come to a satisfactory conclusion you no longer have a say in what happens within the Island Police. Now, we would quite like to carry on with the search if you don't mind."

O'Reilly knew it was pointless arguing. Urban wasn't going to humour him but he didn't know where else to turn. He took his phone back from Urban, looked at the blank screen and started to walk back towards the kitchen.

"Not so fast, Liam," DCI Urban held out his hand. "I need that phone."

"What the hell for?"

"I have made certain allowances because of who you are, but I can only take professional courtesy so far. I know you. I know what you are capable of, and I will not have you jeopardising my investigation by going out on your own private mission. Give me the phone."

O'Reilly handed it over. He knew he had to tread carefully and making an even bigger enemy of Franklin Urban right now wasn't going to do him any favours.

"I'll be in the kitchen if you need me," he said.

He made some more tea and heard the sound of his ringtone in the living room. The ringtone stopped then started again almost immediately.

"To hell with this," O'Reilly put down his tea and went to find DCI Urban. He was now in Assumpta's bedroom. One of his team was looking under the mattress on the bed.

"My daughter has nothing to do with this," O'Reilly said. "Get out of her room."

"That piece of paper you didn't even bother to read gives us the power to search every inch of this apartment," Urban reminded him.

"Who phoned me?" O'Reilly asked.

"Someone called Victoria."

O'Reilly froze. He'd forgotten to tell her what was happening. He really didn't want her to hear about it on the Island grapevine but he feared it was probably already too late. The news would be halfway across the island by now.

"Can I phone her back?" he asked. "She has nothing to do with the Police."

DCI Urban handed him the phone. "You've got two minutes. And I want to listen in to the conversation."

O'Reilly turned his back to the Head of the Border Agency, brought up the most recent calls and quickly forwarded the number Patrick Finney had used to DC Owen's WhatsApp. He added the word, Finney and hoped she would understand what he meant. Then he brought up Victoria Radcliffe's number and pressed, *call*.

She answered straight away. "Liam, are you alright? I heard what happened."

"What have you heard?" he said.

"Someone came in the shop and said you'd been arrested."

"I haven't been arrested. I found a body last night after I left the Snapper and they're just covering all angles. I'm fine."

"You don't sound fine, Liam."

"Have they got any more news about the break in at the shop?" O'Reilly changed the subject. "I've been meaning to call but things have been a bit chaotic on this side of the island."

"Nothing was taken. It's really odd. They had ample time to make off with the stock but they didn't take anything."

"That is odd," O'Reilly agreed but he was already forming a theory about what the break-in at the motorcycle shop was really about.

"Are you sure you're alright?" Victoria said. "Do you want me to come over?"

"I'm fine," O'Reilly said. "I'll make a trip across to Vazon later today. It's all been a big misunderstanding, and it'll blow over in a day or two. The detectives on the new investigating team are sometimes a bit slow on the uptake, that's all."

He turned around and nodded to DCI Urban when he said this. "I'll see you later."

He handed the phone back to Urban.

The DCI yanked it away from him. "Do you think this is a big joke?"

"I don't think it's funny in the slightest," O'Reilly said. "Are you nearly done? I said you wouldn't find anything here, and you haven't, have you?"

"We don't know yet. We'll only know when we've taken what we need back to be tested. You know yourself how long these things can take."

An hour later Urban was satisfied they'd gone over every inch of the apartment. O'Reilly was surprised at how much they'd bagged and were preparing to take back to the lab.

"What's all that?" he pointed to the box full to the brim with evidence bags of all shapes and sizes.

"That is what's called a thorough forensic," DCI Urban said. "We'll be in touch. Don't leave the island."

"Can I have my phone back?"

DCI Urban handed it to him. "Don't do anything stupid. I'll be watching you closely from now on"

O'Reilly suddenly thought of something. He'd been in no fit state to consider it when he'd stumbled upon Delores O'Connell's body, but it hit him now.

"Did you find a chalk drawing at the crime scene?"

"That doesn't concern you anymore," DCI Urban said.

"Did you find a drawing or not? Patrick Finney left them behind at the murder scenes – a crude chalk drawing of a woman with a snake round her neck. He left a number at the bottom of each one."

"I don't recall such a thing, and that's probably because Patrick Finney had nothing to do with Mrs O'Connell's murder. Patrick Finney is nowhere near this island and it's about time you accepted that. Like I said, we'll be in touch."

CHAPTER TWENTY TWO

O'Reilly had to know for certain. He had to make sure there was no chalk drawing anywhere near the spot where Delores O'Connell's body was found. It was going to be risky but he needed to know. He was relying on the fact that Franklin Urban and the Border Agency would be too busy with the items they'd taken from his apartment to pay any more attention to the area outside the Butchers.

O'Reilly decided to walk. He knew he would be less conspicuous that way. The wind was howling again and there were very few people around as he walked. If Patrick Finney was behind all of this O'Reilly knew he would have left something at the scene to let everybody know. He couldn't help himself – he felt a deep-seated need to have his actions acknowledged and O'Reilly hoped this time would be no different.

He reached the Butchers and sighed deeply when he realised there was nobody around. The wind had detached most of the Police tape and now it was flapping around in the gusts. O'Reilly looked behind him for what felt like the hundredth time and approached the place where he'd come across the dead woman the night before.

Crime scenes change as time passes – the blood that has been shed dries out and changes colour and often after some time it's hard to ascertain the brutality that has taken place. There is nothing left to even hint at it. This one was no different, and as O'Reilly scanned the area for what he was looking for he was hit with a strong sense of déjà vu. He wasn't sure if it was because he was here not so long ago or if it was due to something else altogether. He'd lost count of how many times he'd revisited the scene of a crime after the fact and he wondered how many more he would experience.

When Patrick Finney had left his calling card behind in his heyday it was always in an obvious place, in plain view for all to see but as O'Reilly looked around, he couldn't see anything to suggest Ireland's most notorious serial killer had been here at all. It hadn't rained since the murder so if the chalk drawing had been left it would still be visible.

A sound behind him made O'Reilly jump. It was the sound of a car door slamming and soon afterwards O'Reilly heard the chatter of voices getting further and further away. He rubbed his temples and took a step back. He'd been standing almost in exactly the same place last night when someone had emerged from the shadows and hit him on the back of the head. Someone had been hiding, waiting for the moment he came along and found the body.

He turned around and spotted something. There was a narrow access road about ten metres away. The access road ran the whole length of the back of the shops one street away from the esplanade. Against the back walls of the shops were rows of green wheelie bins. This was where the owners of the shops disposed of their rubbish. It was bin day today and most of the bins were full. O'Reilly realised it would be quite possible for someone to crouch between the wheelie bins and stay out of sight. He walked towards them.

He found what he was looking for on the lid of the first bin. The chalk hadn't quite stuck to the plastic of the bin lid in places but it was still quite clear what the drawing depicted. The face of the woman was missing an eye and the snake looked more like a coil of rope that a serpent, but O'Reilly knew this was Patrick Finney's handiwork.

"Why did you draw this on the bin?" he asked himself.

He answered his own question shortly afterwards.

You knew I would come looking, he thought. *You knew I would look for the chalk drawing.*

He stared at it for quite some time. Something was not right about it. O'Reilly remembered the drawing attached to the brick and that's when he saw it. There had been a number at the bottom of the page – the number 5, but the number on this drawing was quite clear. It was so clear in fact that O'Reilly was surprised he didn't spot it first. Whoever had written the number had made sure it was legible. It had been meticulously drawn and gone over again and again. But something was wrong. Something was terribly wrong.

The number written at the bottom of the drawing was the number 6.

* * *

A few miles away in Castel the refuse collectors on that side of the island were looking forward to calling it a day. The gusting winds had made it extremely unpleasant to be outside and had played havoc with the loose bits of rubbish that hadn't been placed in the regulation bags.

"We've just got St George's to do and then it's home time," Lenny Griffin said.

"Thank God for that," his colleague Dan Stewart said.

Dan had only started working as a refuse collector a few weeks ago – it hadn't been as hard as he thought it would be but today was his first taste of the winds that hit the west of the island on the odd occasion.

"They ought to fine them when they don't put the rubbish in the right bags," he commented.

"They're supposed to," Lenny said. "But it's difficult to prove which crap came from which house when the wind blows like this. Anyway, it could be worse – you could be stuck in a poky office all day. At least this gets you out and about."

The refuse truck turned onto St George's and Lenny and Dan got ready to get out.

Lenny pointed to one of the wheelie bins, sticking further out than the others. "They're supposed to put them level with the wall. I bet the neighbours have had something to say about that."

"Who comes up with all these rules?" Dan asked.
"Some bureaucrat with too much time on their hands, I bet. They've probably never done a day on the bins in their lives. Let's get this lot cleared, shall we? It's the wife's birthday today and I promised I'd take her out for a meal."

They were halfway down the street and the two men had worked at record speed. The wind seemed to spur them on.
"One of the wheels is broken on that one," Dan pointed to a bin on the left-hand side of the street. "Shall we leave it?"
"We'll lug it," Lenny told him. "We're not supposed to but you'd be amazed at what going the extra mile does for the Christmas tips. Sometimes we take home a month's salary in tips alone over Christmas. That one belongs to Mrs Dunn and she's always generous with her tips."
"Let's lug it then," Dan agreed.

"Bloody hell," he exclaimed when they tried to drag it towards the back of the refuse truck. "What have they got in here? A dead body?"
"You shouldn't joke about stuff like that," Lenny said. "Put your back into it."
They managed to get it into place at the back of the truck. Lenny shoved it forwards and it came to rest on the hydraulic arm. He pressed the button on the side of the truck and the bin was raised slowly into the air.

Halfway up the lid fell open and a pile of loose rubbish was blown down the road by the wind.
"I knew we should have left it," Dan said. "We're going to have to pick that up now."

A bulging bin liner was next and a split second later two shoes appeared. As the weight of the woman's body forced the rest of her to land in the back of the truck Dan gasped. Lenny saw her too.
"Good Lord," he said and slammed his fist on the red button that stopped the compactor.

Both men dared to peer into the back of the truck. The dead woman was lying on her back on a bed of garbage. Her face was swollen and blue and there was a black scab across the entire length of her neck.

As Dan Stewart lost his lunch on the road he vowed never again to joke about dead bodies. Neither Dan Stewart or Lenny Griffin had noticed the chalk drawing on the lid of the bin – it was a crude depiction of a woman with a snake coiled round her neck. At the bottom of the picture someone had written the number, 5.

CHAPTER TWENTY THREE

"A wheelie bin?" DS Skinner said.

"It's the first one you can see from the road," O'Reilly told him. "Finney has left his calling card on the lid of a wheelie bin."

O'Reilly had debated whether to get hold of DCI Urban and tell him what he'd found but, in the end, he'd decided to phone the switchboard at the station and ask to be put through to someone in his own team. Urban would no doubt want to know what he was doing snooping around at the scene of a crime he was a suspect in.

"Go and take a look," O'Reilly continued. "Get hold of Jim Peters and get over there."

"This isn't our party anymore, sir," DS Skinner reminded him.

"I'm well aware of that. I'm well aware the party has been gate-crashed by a bunch of idiots, but you need to check that bin."

"What about Urban?" Skinner asked. "What do we tell him?"

"I couldn't give a rat's arse what you tell him, Will. Tell him you found it by chance. Tell him the owner of the bin was a Paddy Finney fan and recognised the calling card. This is the work of Finney and that chalk drawing proves it."

O'Reilly realised he was shaking when he'd ended the call. He took a few deep breaths and sat down on a nearby bench. He felt like he was the only one on the island who actually knew what was going on. Patrick Finney was in Guernsey and he was hell-bent on destroying O'Reilly's life and nobody seemed to believe him. Nobody could see what was happening and O'Reilly knew he was running out of both time and options.

Patrick Finney had been caught before but at what cost? O'Reilly had been on the brink of losing everything because of his determination to bring Finney down. His marriage had almost collapsed because of it – his wife

Mary had used the word obsession on more than one occasion and he'd been lucky to come out of it with his sanity intact.

Would he be able to go through all that again, this time with nobody to help him? He didn't think he could. He would need some help to beat Finney again, but he didn't know how to get that help when none of his colleagues or friends knew what a monster Finney actually was nor did they understand the way his mind operated.

As O'Reilly sat and stared out to sea a thought entered his mind. It was an idea so repulsive it made him shiver. He realised there was someone who might be able to help him – someone who knew Finney inside out, but asking this man for help could have repercussions that might be considerably worse than the predicament he was currently in. He pushed the idea aside. He would try and sort this out on his own for the time being. He would reconsider his options only when he had no other choice.

The wind was showing no sign of easing off as O'Reilly walked back towards his apartment. He almost took a right onto La Grange out of habit. This was the way he usually walked to the station, but there was no way he would be able to show his face there right now. He'd promised Victoria he would come across to Vazon, and the more he thought about it the more it sounded like the best thing to do. He needed to get away from the capital for a while. He needed time to think and consider his next move.

Assumpta wasn't home when O'Reilly went inside the apartment. He put some more food in Bram's bowl, picked up his car keys and left again, making sure to lock the front door.

The roads were busier than he expected them to be and it took him thirty minutes to drive a distance he usually covered in half that time. It was just after four and Radcliffe Bikes would still be open for another hour, so he parked down the road from the shop and got out of the car.

The bike shop was quiet. Victoria was talking to her brother, Tommy behind the counter. For once Tommy offered O'Reilly a smile. It had taken a while for Victoria's brother to warm to the Irish detective – O'Reilly hadn't pushed the matter, but now Tommy seemed to accept that O'Reilly was a permanent part of his sister's life, and he was much more civil than he had been at the beginning.

"Liam," Victoria came round the side of the counter and gave him a hug. "It's terrible what's happened. How are you?"

"Grand," O'Reilly said. "Any news about the break-in?"

"They broke the lock at the back," Tommy told him. "The back of the yard where we keep the bikes that are in for repair, but they didn't take anything. Perhaps they were disturbed."

"Perhaps," O'Reilly repeated.

He didn't believe this for a second. He was becoming more and more convinced the break-in was Patrick Finney's doing. Finney used this as a ruse to get Victoria out of the picture and leave O'Reilly on his own. It was simple – with Victoria called away O'Reilly would soon leave and that's when Finney struck.

"We've fixed the lock anyway," Victoria said. "Are you hungry?"

"I could eat something," O'Reilly replied.

"Get off home," Tommy said to his sister. "I can lock up.

"Thanks, Tommy," Victoria said. "I'll see you tomorrow."

"Take the day off. It's been dead quiet recently – I'm sure I can manage on my own."

"I'm taking a week off next month," Victoria reminded him.

"Take tomorrow off. From what I heard Liam isn't going to be at work for a while."

"What exactly have you heard?" O'Reilly asked him.

"Something about you being arrested for the murder of that old tramp in the capital."

"I haven't been arrested. If I had I wouldn't be standing here now. I found the body and the first thing we do in any murder investigation is look into the life of the one who finds the body. It's as simple as that."

"I'm just telling you what's going around."

"Perhaps you shouldn't pay so much attention to the wagging tongues on the island," O'Reilly turned to Victoria. "Shall we go?"

CHAPTER TWENTY FOUR

"He said it was on the lid of a wheelie bin," DS Skinner said.

"A wheelie bin?" DC Owen repeated.

She, DS Skinner and DC Andy Stone were standing by the front desk at the station.

"There's a service road at the back of the shops close to where the woman's body was found," DS Skinner continued. "The DI said the chalk drawing is on the lid of the first one. He reckons it was Patrick Finney's calling card when he killed all those women."

"A wheelie bin?" DC Stone said.

"That's what he said."

"We should go and check," DC Owen said.

"It's not our concern," DS Skinner said. "We'll be in deep trouble if we go snooping around in an investigation the GBA have taken over."

"Urban will have our balls," DC Stone added.

"We need to go and see what's on that wheelie bin," DC Owen was adamant.

"What was that about a wheelie bin?"

None of them had realised that DCI Franklin Urban had approached the desk.

"Tell him," DC Owen said to DS Skinner.

"Tell me what?" Urban said.

DS Skinner sighed. "I got a phone call from DI O'Reilly, sir."

"Go on."

"He's convinced that Patrick Finney killed that woman last night, sir. He knew there would be a chalk drawing somewhere at the scene, so he went to take a look and he found it. It was a drawing of a woman with a snake round her neck and there was a number at the bottom. It was Finney's calling card when he killed all those women in Dublin."

"Do I need to remind you that O'Reilly is a suspect in this murder?" Urban addressed all three of them.

"You can't honestly believe he killed that woman, sir?" It was DC Owen.

"You are to stay away from this investigation. Do I make myself clear?"

"Perfectly, sir," DS Skinner said.

"I still think you should check that wheelie bin, sir," DC Owen wasn't giving up. "The DI wouldn't make up something like that."

"Leave it be, DC Owen," Urban ordered. "Now, if there's nothing else, I have more pressing matters to attend to."

"You shouldn't push him," DC Stone said to DC Owen when DCI Urban had gone. "He can be a nasty bastard when he wants to be."

"He doesn't scare me," DC Owen said. "My dad warned me about him when I joined up but the likes of Franklin Urban don't scare me."

"He scares the crap out of me," DS Skinner admitted.

The phone started to ring behind the desk. PC London answered it. The three detectives watched as her facial expression changed. Her eyes widened and her mouth opened.

"Where was this?" she asked.

Her mouth opened wider still.

"I'll log it and get somebody there as soon as possible."

She looked up at Skinner, Owen and Stone and shook her head.

"What's wrong, Kim?" DS Skinner asked.

"We've got another body, Sarge," she said. "Over in Castel. Two refuse collectors found the body of a woman in a wheelie bin?"

"A wheelie bin?" DC Owen and DC Stone said at the same time.

"They were emptying it into the truck when a woman's body fell out of the bin."

"I'll get hold of DCI Fish," DS Skinner said. "What on earth is going on here?"

* * *

"Do you think this has something to do with the woman killed last night?" DC Stone asked as they drove across the island to Castel.

"Why would it be?" DC Owen said.

"Two words, Katie. Wheelie bin. They have to be connected. And the DI is in the frame for the O'Connell woman. Perhaps O'Reilly is a closet serial killer."

"That's not funny, Andy."

"That's enough, you two," DCI Fish said. "We're probably looking at two completely unconnected incidents here, and I'll have no more talk of DI O'Reilly."

"He's being treated really badly, sir," DC Owen said. "How can they even think he killed that woman?"

"Urban is going on the evidence alone, Katie. That's all. He doesn't know DI O'Reilly like we do, and that's precisely why we've been taken off the case. It stinks but it is what it is. What's the address again?"

"Number 18 St George's, sir," DC Stone told him.

An ambulance was already parked on the side of the road when they got there. Two Police cars were parked on either side of a green refuse truck. Two PCs were busy sealing the area around it with Police tape. DCI Fish parked behind them.

"Has Peters been informed?" DC Stone asked DCI Fish as they got out of the car.

"He's on his way. Let's go and have a look, shall we? Then I want to speak to the two refuse collectors who found the body. And I want those people out of the way."

He pointed to the small crowd of people who had already gathered behind the Police cars.

"I'll get onto it, sir," DC Stone offered.

The refuse truck looked brand new. The shiny green paintwork was spotless. DCI Fish nodded to the two PCs and he and DC Owen ducked underneath the tape.

The first thing both detectives realised was the woman lying on the rubbish bags had been dead for quite some time. Her face had taken on a bluish-grey tinge and the skin was blistered in places. Bloating had already begun, and the unmistakable stench of putrefaction had overpowered the reek of the garbage. Flies were buzzing around the dried pus on the eyes and mouth. Maggots had already hatched and were milling around in the jagged gash on the neck.

"Not a pretty sight," DCI Fish commented.

DC Owen remained silent. Her gaze was fixed on the dead woman.

"Katie," DCI Fish said. "Are you alright?"

"What?" DC Owen said. "Yes, I'm fine."

She'd seen her fair share of dead bodies but it was something she knew she would never get used to.

Jim Peters appeared with DS Henry Earle in tow.

"Sorry it took so long," the Head of Forensics said. "What have we got?"

DCI Fish pointed to the dead woman.

"She's been dead for a while," Peters said. "Look at the bloating."

"What do you reckon?" DCI Fish said.

"Pathology will give us more," Peters looked more closely at the body. "But three days at least, probably longer. Looks like she had her throat slit."

"We'll leave you to it then. The coroner has been informed. Katie, let's see what the refuse collectors can tell us."

Lenny Griffin and Dan Stewart were speaking to a couple of paramedics further down the road. Lenny had his hand on Dan's shoulder. The younger man didn't look healthy at all – his face was deathly pale and there were specks of vomit on his uniform. DCI Fish and DC Owen walked up to them.

Fish took out his ID. "DCI Fish and this is DC Owen from the Island Police. I believe it was you who found the body?"

"I've never seen anything like it," Lenny said. "I've been working the bins for over twenty years and I've never seen anything like this before."

"Did you recognise the woman?"

"Never seen her before. What a thing to find in a wheelie bin."

"Who owns the bin she was in?" DC Owen asked.

"Mrs Dunn from number 18," Lenny said. "Lovely old duck."

Dan Stewart started to shake. His whole body trembled as though he had a fever.

"You should get yourself checked out," DC Owen said. "You're probably in shock."

"The paramedics have had a look at him," Lenny said. "He refused to go to hospital."

"I'm fine," Dan managed. "Did you see her face? The maggots?"

"Get yourself to the hospital," DCI Fish said. "Shock is nothing to play around with."

"He's right, Dan," Lenny said. "I'll help you up."

He held out his hand and led Dan towards the ambulance.

"What do you think?" DC Owen said.

"I don't know what to think, Katie. The bins are collected once a week, so whoever dumped her in the wheelie bin either kept the body somewhere after they killed her or she's been in that bin for quite some time. Let's go and speak to Mrs Dunn at number 18, shall we?"

CHAPTER TWENTY FIVE

"How are you really, Liam?" Victoria asked O'Reilly.

"I've been better to be honest," he replied.

They were sitting at the table in the dining room in her house. O'Reilly was already halfway through his second beer.

"What actually happened?" Victoria said.

"When you left the Snapper last night that drunk woman walked up and grabbed me. I shook her off but she was so sozzled she fell to the ground. I told her to leave and she did. Then when I was walking home, I found her outside the Butchers with her throat slit."

"That's terrible."

"It gets worse. While I was checking to see if she was alright someone attacked me from behind. I must have blacked out for a second because when I woke up, I was on top of the woman with a knife in my hand."

"Oh my God. Are you alright?"

"I've had worse. But now I'm a suspect. I've been questioned and earlier today I had a whole load of forensics officers ransacking my apartment."

"Surely they can't do that?" Victoria said. "You're a detective inspector for Pete's sake. I can't believe your team have treated you like that."

"It wasn't my team," O'Reilly drained the beer in his glass. "The case has been handed over to the Border Agency and the lead detective there isn't my biggest fan. Let's just say we share a bit of a history. I've been well and truly set up."

"Who on earth would do such a thing?"

"I need another drink. I'll get us a refill and I'll tell you all about it."

He returned soon afterwards with two more beers and an obese white cat in tow.

"The cat seems to like me," he said.

"Shadow doesn't like many people," Victoria said. "You were going to tell me all about it."

O'Reilly handed her a beer and sat back down. "Fifteen years ago, Dublin was terrorised by a man by the name of Patrick Finney. He killed women by the light of the full moon. For four months he held the city in his grip. Women were afraid to go out at night and the Police didn't seem to be any closer to catching him."

"I think I read something about it at the time," Victoria said.

"Finney was Ireland's most notorious serial killer. And he was incredibly clever and meticulously careful. He didn't leave anything behind and he changed his MO every time. But he made a mistake. Two actually. His first mistake was killing one of my friends and colleagues. Ellie Finch was her name. She was a DC and she had a bright future ahead of her. She was one in a million, was Ellie – bright and kind-hearted with it. She wasn't unlike Katie Owen actually. Anyway, when Finney murdered her, I took it personally. I worked night and day and I didn't stop. It almost cost me everything I had, but I couldn't let Ellie down. Then, one night I found something. Something we'd overlooked at first. Finney had left something behind."

"What did he leave behind?"

"His ego caused him to slip up," O'Reilly said. "Ellie had been working on the case notes the time she was killed and Finney found them. The arrogant bastard had the cheek to correct them. He crossed out the bits that were wrong. That's how I got him. His prints were on the red pen he used. He was on the system, and we arrested him the next day. He was sent down for life with no chance of parole."

"And you think someone close to this Finney character is out for revenge?"

"No," O'Reilly said. "It's Finney who wants revenge. He's out, Victoria and he's here on the island. He's hell-bent on ruining my life and so far, he's doing a good job of it."

"I thought you said he was in jail for life," Victoria said.

"He escaped last week and he's come here for me."

"I don't mean to doubt you, but how can you be so sure it's him?"

"He's been sending me signals to warn me," O'Reilly said. "Stuff he knows I'll know are from him and today he actually phoned me. He phoned me while I had a house full of forensics officers. He's watching me, I can feel it."

Shadow jumped up on the chair next to O'Reilly's. Considering her impressive bulk, she was rather graceful in doing so.

"Shadow," Victoria reprimanded. "That's very rude."

"She's alright," O'Reilly said. "I've got used to the bad manners of cats. Bram has the manners of an ape, but he's grown on me."

"What are you going to do?" Victoria's tone turned serious. "About this Patrick Finney thing. Have you told your superiors about him?"

"Nobody believes me," O'Reilly said. "And Finney has done a good job of covering his tracks. Nothing he's done so far can be linked back to him, so I'm pretty much on my own."

"You're not on your own. You've got me and Assumpta."

"I don't want either of you involved," O'Reilly placed his hand on hers. "Paddy Finney is evil and I don't want you or Summi to get involved."

"What do you feel like eating?" Victoria asked. "I can rustle up some steak and potatoes."

"Sounds grand. I'll get us some more drinks."

* * *

"Mrs Dunn," DCI Fish said. "We're from the Island Police. Can we have a word?"

Mrs Dunn looked Fish and DC Owen up and down. She had to be knocking on for eighty but her eyes were bright and alert.
"Island Police?" she said. "Have I done something wrong?"
"Of course not," DC Owen told her. "We just need to ask you a few questions about your wheelie bin."
Mrs Dunn smiled at her. "Nothing surprises me anymore. You'd better come in. I'll put the kettle on."

DCI Fish helped himself to a custard cream. "Mrs Dunn – where do you keep your wheelie bin when it's not bin day?"
She pointed to the plate of biscuits. "I usually make my own, but you've come on the wrong day. If you'd been two days earlier there would have been some coconut macaroons left, but Mr Green at number 12 has developed quite a taste for them. My wheelie bin, you say?"
"That's right," DC Owen said.
"It's kept by the gate in the back yard. That way I don't have to push it too far to where they collect it. The old back isn't what it used to be. I'll be eighty next month, you know."
"You look great for it," DC Owen said.
"Is the gate locked?" DCI Fish asked.
She frowned at him. "Of course not. I've never had any trouble before."
"When did you last open the bin?" DC Owen said.
"What's this all about?" Mrs Dunn asked.
"We're not quite sure," DCI Fish didn't want to tell her too much. "When the bin men were emptying your bin, they found something that shouldn't have been in there. When did you last open the bin?"
"There's not so much rubbish now, what with my Ken passing. I think I last took the bin bags out on Friday."
DC Owen did some quick mental arithmetic. Today was Monday so she hadn't been near the bin for three days."

"Mrs Dunn," DCI Fish said. "Have you noticed anyone hanging around in the last few days?"

"Hanging around?"

"Someone who seemed out of place?" DC Owen elaborated.

Mrs Dunn took a small sip of her tea. "There was something that seemed odd to me."

"Go on," DCI Fish urged.

"A man," the elderly lady said. "I was hanging some washing out on the weekend and I noticed this man lingering across the road."

"Did you recognise this man?" DCI Fish asked.

"I only saw him from the back, but even then I knew I hadn't seen him before."

"What do you mean when you say he was lingering?" DC Owen asked.

"His body language told me he was up to no good. I used to work in the job centre and I soon learned to spot people's intentions by reading their body language. You know what I mean – you can tell if someone is genuinely out looking for work or if they're just there to get the dole money. Anyway, this man was up to something."

"What did this man look like?" DCI Fish said. "From behind, I mean?"

"Shifty. His head was bowed like he didn't want anyone to see him. He had brown hair and he wasn't that tall." She looked over to DC Owen. "He wasn't much taller than you, love. And he was quite portly."

"What was he wearing?" DC Owen asked.

"A brown coat and a pair of black trousers. I'm sorry I can't be of more help. I didn't see his face I'm afraid."

"You've been a great help," DC Owen said.

DCI Fish handed her one of his cards. "If you see him again, please give me a call. You can call the station or on my mobile number. Any time."

"What's he done?" Mrs Dunn asked as the two detectives were leaving. "This man I saw, what do you think he's done?"

"We're not sure yet," DC Owen said. "Call us if you see this man again."

"Pop round on Friday," Mrs Dunn said. "I'll have a fresh batch of macaroons to offer you then."

"They sound delicious. Thank you for your time."

CHAPTER TWENTY SIX

"That was delicious," O'Reilly put down his knife and fork. "That has to be the best steak I've eaten in a long while."

Victoria looked across at his empty plate. "So I see. Having the weight of the world on your shoulders doesn't appear to have affected your appetite."

"It never has done," O'Reilly said. "When the going gets tough the tough Irish eat food."

"You're a tough guy, then?"

"It has been said. And right now, this tough guy is going to work off some of that food by washing the dishes."

"I've got a dishwasher, Liam," she reminded him. "It can wait. Tell me more about this Finney character. Let's sit somewhere more comfortable."

"Paddy Finney is a monster," O'Reilly said.

He sat next to Victoria in the living room. "A monster like no other I've ever come across. His first victim was a young university student. Her roommate found her in the bath with her throat sliced open so badly she was in danger of being decapitated."

"How did he manage to get into her bathroom?"

"Finney has charm," O'Reilly took a deep breath. "And he was a good-looking man back then. It wasn't hard for him to get his victims where he wanted them."

"Why did he kill? Sorry for all the questions."

"It's alright. His motive, if you can call it that was the moon deserved sacrifice and it was his responsibility to offer that sacrifice. He only killed under the light of the full moon. He chose each victim carefully. When we got there, I could see why he'd chosen that particular place – the bathroom window was huge and the full moon would have shone in and lit up the place beautifully."

"He sounds like a real madman."

"His defence suggested they go the insanity route but Finney was having none of it. He was articulate and he had an answer for everything. He knew exactly what he was doing and his reasoning, albeit a sick one was deemed to be within the bounds of sanity by the judge who passed sentence."

"He doesn't sound sane to me."

"He's a psychopath," O'Reilly said. "And he told me he would have carried on killing if I hadn't caught him."

"I'll fix us some more drinks," Victoria said.

She came back with two beers. "There's one thing I don't understand."

"What's that?" O'Reilly said.

"Why risk coming to the island to get you? It doesn't make any sense."

"Paddy Finney's actions have never made any sense. I think he blames me for stopping him."

"But you weren't the one who sentenced him to life," Victoria pointed out.

"I was the one who caught him. I was the one who put a stop to his sick rituals. Fifteen years behind bars is a long time to think of a way to get revenge."

"Don't jump down my throat, Liam," Victoria said. "But what if you're wrong? What if the death of the woman you found has nothing to do with Finney?"

"It was him."

"Please, hear me out. What if it was someone else altogether? They could have killed her and heard you coming."

"No, that doesn't fit. They wouldn't have stuck around – they would have legged it, not bashed me over the head. This was Finney – he's on the island and he's out for revenge. Can we talk about something else? Where in the Canary Islands did you have in mind?"

His mobile phone started to ring before Victoria had a chance to reply. He debated whether to ignore it but realised it could be Assumpta.

"I need to see who it is," he told Victoria and went to fetch the phone.

It wasn't his daughter it was DC Owen.

"Katie," he answered it. "Is everything alright?"

"I don't know, sir," she said.

Her voice sounded muffled. She sounded like she was talking with something covering her mouth.

"I can't hear you," O'Reilly said. "Where are you?"

"I'm in the Ladies at the station, sir. I didn't want anyone to overhear."

"What's going on, Katie?"

"We've got another body," she told him. "Some bin men found it in a wheelie bin earlier today."

"I've been taken off the team, Katie," he said. "What exactly is it you want me to do about it?"

"DI Peters sent through an initial forensic on the bin, sir. He found a chalk drawing on the lid. It was exactly the same as the one you described. The one on the bin close to where Delores O'Connell was found."

O'Reilly suddenly felt numb. "Did you see the drawing?"

"I only saw a photo of it, sir. It was pretty childlike if you ask me."

O'Reilly had to ask. He had to know.

"Was there a number at the bottom?"

"How did you know?"

"Because I know Patrick Finney. What was the number?"

"It was the number 5."

"The number on the first bin I found was the number six," O'Reilly said.

"Delores O'Connell was killed after the woman the bin men found."

"There's more, sir," DC Owen said. "We're off the investigation once more. In light of the discovery of the drawing on the bin, Urban had a change of heart and went back to the first murder scene. He found the other chalk drawing and now he believes the two murders are connected."

"Of course they're bloody connected, Katie. My cat could see they're connected. They're connected to Patrick Finney and that's what Urban and his team need to realise."

"The whole thing has been handed over. Peters was furious when Urban stormed in and told him the news. He had to let Urban's team carry on with the forensic."

The line went quiet for a moment.

"Katie," O'Reilly said. "Are you still there?"

"I thought I heard someone coming in, sir," she said.

"Why exactly are you phoning me from the toilets?"

"Because..." She stopped there.

"Katie," O'Reilly urged.

"Urban is looking for you, sir," DC Owen continued.

"He knows where to find me."

"You don't understand. DCI Fish and I spoke to the old lady whose wheelie bin the latest body was in, and she told us she noticed a man hanging around her back alley. It was a man she hadn't seen before and she said he was acting suspiciously."

"It was Finney," O'Reilly said. "This is all Finney's doing."

"You don't understand, sir," DC Owen said. "The man she described matched your description."

"You can't be serious?"

"She only saw him from the back, but he was your height and build and he had the same colour hair. She even described the jacket and trousers he was wearing. They're the same as the ones you sometimes wear, sir."

O'Reilly couldn't believe what he was hearing.

"Why are you telling me all this, Katie?"

"Because I know you couldn't kill those women, sir," she said. "I know you could never do something like that, but DCI Urban doesn't share my opinion and he's going to come looking for you."

"You need to stop right there, Katie. I appreciate the heads-up, but you could get into serious trouble for this."

"But you're innocent."

"It doesn't matter. Don't call me again. I'll figure something out."

CHAPTER TWENTY SEVEN

"Do you realise what time it is?"
DCI Franklin Urban wasn't impressed. No sooner had he settled down in front of the TV to watch a series he'd been following on Netflix his phone had started to ring. DI Rob Crown was a man of few words but the forensic officer's voice was animated as he explained to Urban what he'd found. He'd also insisted that the Head of the Border Agency needed to see it for himself.

It was an hour before midnight and now DCI Urban was standing next to his colleague in the lab.

"I know it's late, sir," DI Crown said. "But I found something very interesting."

"Go on."

Crown pointed to something on the screen of his laptop.

"What am I supposed to be looking at?" Urban asked.

"That is the cross-section of one of the fibres from the jumper the woman was wearing, sir. It's mohair – very expensive and very unique. And the fibres are easily detached if they come into contact with other items of clothing."

"Did you call me out in the middle of the night to educate me on the virtues and pitfalls of mohair?"

DI Crown ignored him and tapped the mouse pad to bring up another, almost identical image.

"Something clicked when I saw it, sir," he said. "Something I thought was odd earlier."

"They're the same cross-sections, Crown," DCI Urban said.

"That's because both strands came from the same mohair jumper, sir. And the strand on the left wasn't pulled from the jumper the woman was wearing – it was found on a pair of trousers we picked up from DI O'Reilly's apartment. The trousers and a jacket were scrunched up on the floor of the bathroom and both items of clothing were covered in the stuff."

DCI Urban was suddenly interested. "Are you absolutely positive?"

"Ninety-five percent sure, sir."

"I knew it," Urban said. "We've got him."

"I still find it hard to believe, sir."

"Not everything makes sense, Rob. I knew there was something not right about that Irishman the moment he set foot on this island. What else have you found?"

"Nothing yet, sir. I concentrated on the mohair when I realised I'd seen similar fibres on O'Reilly's clothes."

"They're not similar, Rob," Urban said. "You said it yourself, they're identical. Good work. Let me know if you find anything else."

Urban stepped out into the fresh night air with a rare smile on his face. There was no way the irritating Irish detective would be able to talk his way out of this one. Two women had been found dead – identical chalk drawings had been found close to both murder scenes and all the evidence pointed to Liam O'Reilly. He'd been found at the first scene covered in blood. His fingerprints were on the knife used to kill the woman, and witnesses had confirmed he'd got into an altercation with her earlier that evening.

A man matching his description was seen acting strangely close to where the second victim ended up, and now they had proof that O'Reilly had come into contact with the dead woman in the form of fibres from a very distinct mohair jumper. As far as Urban was concerned it was game, set and match for Detective Inspector Liam O'Reilly.

He wondered whether to arrange for a team to go and pick him up now – surprise him in the dead of night, but he decided against it. O'Reilly would be none the wiser by the morning anyway. His team had been kept in the dark and none of them were aware of the new developments. No, Urban would give the jumped-up Irish detective an early-morning wake-up call and throw the evidence they had against him then.

Urban got in his car and drove home. Tomorrow was going to be a really great day.

* * *

A few miles across the island in Vazon Patrick Duncan Finney was immersed in a terrible internal conflict. Again and again, he'd debated the pros and cons of what he was about to do and couldn't make up his mind one way or the other. It had been two days since the full moon and already the glorious orb in the sky above was starting to wane. It wasn't right, but there wouldn't be another full moon for weeks and he knew he couldn't wait that long. He had to make up his mind soon.

He gazed skywards – the waning gibbous was talking to him, but the words from the moon weren't the words he wanted to hear from her. He tried a change of tack – a change of rationale to reassure himself he was making the right decision. This wasn't about the moon anymore. This wasn't about sacrifice. This was about revenge.

Fifteen years isn't an awful long time in the greater scheme of things. Even when he dissected the time into days Finney realised the five and a half thousand he'd spent in the secure unit of Portlaoise was a mere pinprick on the graph of time.

But a man can still do a lot of thinking in fifteen years. Finney's time in Portlaoise wasn't entirely unpleasant – held in isolation for much of the time he didn't have much to do with the other inmates and he was left alone with his books and his thoughts. Liam O'Reilly occupied a lot of them and after a decade and a half behind bars Finney knew the Irish detective was the reason the moon looked different now. Fifteen years – 180 full moons. It sounded impossible but the more he thought about it the more Finney realised it could be done.

The two days spent in the medical wing after an attack he didn't see coming opened his eyes to a possibility he'd never considered before. There was a chance of redemption – a second chance where he would be able to kill two birds with one stone. His lover the moon would be appeased and his nemesis would be broken in two.

O'Reilly wouldn't find a way back from this but first the woman in the window of the second-floor apartment would have to become an unwilling accomplice. The moon didn't shine so bright now but Patrick Finney didn't seem to notice.

CHAPTER TWENTY EIGHT

The sound of O'Reilly's mobile phone became part of a dream he was having. In the dream two-headed serpents were taunting him and slithering around his feet. Suddenly the hideous asps rose to the sound of music and began to dance. It would have been comical if it weren't so macabre – scores of two-headed snakes jiving to the lively sounds of Whiskey in the Jar.

O'Reilly pushed the dream aside and reached out for his phone before the voicemail kicked in. Victoria Radcliffe was snoring quietly in the bed next to him. O'Reilly saw from the screen it was his daughter.

"Summi," he answered it. "Is everything alright?"

"No."

That one word made O'Reilly sit up in bed. He carefully removed the duvet, picked up his clothes and left the room. The creek of the hinges on the bedroom door caused Victoria to stir but she didn't wake.

"What's happened?" O'Reilly asked Assumpta downstairs.

"The Police were here again, Dad," she told him. "That arrogant Border bloke."

"Franklin Urban," O'Reilly said. "What did he want?"

"He wanted to know where you were, and he didn't believe me when I said I didn't know. Where are you? At Victoria's?"

"It's best you don't know, Summi. I'm in a lot of trouble. Katie phoned me last night and gave me a heads-up. Urban is coming for me and if he finds me, I know for a fact that he'll arrest me. What did you say to him?"

"The truth," Assumpta said. "I told him I hadn't seen you since yesterday afternoon and I didn't know where you had gone."

"He's going to come here. It's only a matter of time before he finds me here."

"How are we going to sort this mess out, Dad?"

"*We're* not," O'Reilly told her. "I am. I don't want you involved in any of this. Paddy Finney isn't going to stop until he's caught and I'm running out of options."

"What's that supposed to mean?"

"It means desperate times call for desperate measures, Summi. The Police aren't an option anymore, so I have to go to Plan B. I didn't want to go that route but I can't see any other way out of this."

"You're scaring me now, Dad. What are you going to do?"

"I'm going to sell my soul to the devil. I have no other choice. It would be better if you don't contact me again. I have to get off the radar for a while and for all I know Urban is tracking your calls."

"You're not going to do anything stupid are you?"

"I'm afraid I am, Summi," O'Reilly said. "I'm about to something extremely stupid. I'll sort everything out. Don't worry about me."

He rang off and stared at the blank screen of his phone. He knew he had to get rid of it. The clock on the wall told him it was not yet six in the morning. He couldn't believe Urban and his gang had gone to his apartment so early.

He opened the back door and walked down the path to the gate at the bottom. An early-riser in the house next door was busy locking the front door. Before the young woman turned around O'Reilly took out his phone and slid it through the gap in the back window of her car. She'd left it open. He felt a pang of guilt as he did so – he knew there was a possibility she would have to endure the company of Franklin Urban during the course of the day but O'Reilly needed to get that phone as far away from him as he could. He walked back up the path and heard the car driving away as he went inside the house.

Victoria was making coffee in the kitchen.

"You're up early," she said. "Tea?"

"I have to go," O'Reilly said.

"I never had you pegged as a love 'em and leave 'em kind of man."

O'Reilly kissed her on the cheek. "I'm not."

He told her about the phone call from Assumpta.

"They'll be looking for me," he said. "And they'll find out about you sooner or later."

"Where are you going to go?" Victoria asked.

"I don't know yet. It's better that you don't know. I've got rid of my phone so you won't be able to contact me but that's for the best too. I need to sort this mess out."

"I can help you, you know."

"I know, but I don't want you to. I'd better get going. It's only a matter of time before Urban turns up and if that happens, I'm finished."

He left his car parked outside Victoria's house. He knew they would be looking for it and he would be better off on foot. He didn't know where he was going to go, but he did know he needed to make a few phone calls. They were calls he was dreading but he knew there was only one person he could turn to right now.

The Man was an enigma back in Ireland. Very few people had ever seen his face and many believed he didn't actually exist. He operated so far off the radar that the Garda had all but given up trying to bring him down. He controlled the majority of the drug trade in the capital and it was estimated he had his hand in over eighty percent of illicit activities in and around Dublin.

Very often when the need arose The Man would diversify and tread on feet. But more often than not, when The Man trod on your feet those feet stayed trodden on. Nobody dared to go up against The Man if they knew what was best for them and those that did were made to regret it.

But O'Reilly knew another side to this phantom – a side hardly anybody got to see and it was this side of him he was hoping to use to his advantage now. The Man had a deep-rooted sense of justice – a perverse moralistic side that only served to make him more and more difficult to fathom out. He truly was an enigma in the murky depths of the Dublin underground. He'd been responsible for more murders than anyone else in the history of organised crime in Ireland yet he refused to harm a woman or a child. Rumour had it he'd once bequeathed the entire profits from a lucrative operation to a children's home in the city. The Man was a true contradiction in terms – a phantom with many faces yet only a select few had ever laid eyes on his true face.

O'Reilly knew it wasn't going to be easy to get in touch with The Man but he still had a few contacts back in his home town and he hoped and prayed they would be willing to help. The first thing he needed to do was get hold of another phone. He needed a pre-paid one that would take much longer to trace than his old contract one. He came up with a plan. It was the first step on the way to getting the train on the track and he knew for a fact that once that train was set in motion it would be impossible to stop.

He found what he was looking for outside a small shopping mall in Vazon central. A couple of youths were hanging around waiting for something to happen. The two boys were in their late-teens and both looked extremely bored.

O'Reilly looked around and walked over to them. He took out his ID and made sure both of the youths knew what they were looking at.

"We're not doing anything," the taller of the two said.

"I can see that," O'Reilly said. "I actually need your help."

"What are you talking about?" the shorter boy asked.

O'Reilly nodded to one of the shops. Island Cellular was a small shop with a grubby façade. The windows looked like they hadn't been washed in a very long time.

"I'm working with the Border Agency."

O'Reilly had thought that part up on the spur of the moment.

"And we're investigating illegals coming to the island and disappearing off the radar."

"We're not illegals," the taller youth said.

"I didn't say you were. What I need your help with is this: often when these immigrants get here, they manage to get hold of mobile phones that aren't on the system. The sims are not registered."

"Pre-paid," the short youth had cottoned on.

"That's right," O'Reilly said. "And we've been keeping an eye on Island Cellular. We have reason to believe they're charging way above what they should for these phones."

"What's that got to do with us?"

"We need proof. I could go in there and try and buy an illegal phone, but they'll smell a rat straight away. Whereas..."

He waited. He didn't have to wait long.

"If one of us goes in there they'll probably sell it to us no questions asked." It was the shorter boy. He was clearly quicker on the uptake than his lanky friend.

"I'm not talking top of the range," O'Reilly took out his wallet and handed the boy four fifty-pound notes. "See what you can get with that. Airtime too. I'll need airtime. You can keep the change."

The short youth looked at his friend and nodded. They both turned around and headed for Island Cellular.

They returned a short while later with a carrier bag. The short youth handed it to O'Reilly and the Irish DI looked inside.

"Piece of cake," the boy said. "It cost fifty quid more than normal but we got a decent Samsung and twenty quid of airtime and the same amount of data."

He took out two twenty-pound notes and offered them to O'Reilly.

"I said you could have it. Thanks, lads – you've helped out the Border Agency no end. I'd appreciate it if you kept this to yourselves for the time being. We're getting close to a breakthrough and we need to be careful."

"Cool," the tall youth said.

"Let's go," his friend said. "We can get that new X-Box game now."

CHAPTER TWENTY NINE

DCI Franklin Urban was in a foul mood. All attempts to locate O'Reilly had failed and he wasn't sure what to do. He'd tried O'Reilly's apartment, he'd looked for him at Victoria Radcliffe's house in Vazon and he'd even ordered one of his team to search every inch of the station in the hope that O'Reilly was hiding out there, but he'd come up empty-handed. O'Reilly's service provider had informed them the trace on his mobile phone was going to take time.

"This is extremely frustrating," Urban addressed his team in the briefing room. "But it can't be helped. We'll find him – Guernsey is a small island and there aren't many places to hide, but what I'd like to do is recap on what we have so far. Delores O'Connell was killed on Monday night outside the Butchers shop on La Grange. O'Reilly claimed he came across her body on the way home from a restaurant. He was covered in Mrs O'Connell's blood and his fingerprints were found on the knife that was used to kill her. O'Reilly also claimed he was attacked and woke up on top of Mrs O'Connell with the knife in his hand. This is how he explained the blood and the fingerprints on the knife. Now, I cannot be the only one in this room who can see how far-fetched this sounds. Earlier, witnesses claim O'Reilly was involved in an altercation with the dead woman and it seems that they were acquainted back in Ireland. We simply cannot afford to ignore all the evidence against him. Detective Inspector or not, it is quite clear he was involved in the murder of that poor woman and we will bring him in during the course of the day."

"He was interviewed already, wasn't he?" DS Carl Rowland said. "Why wasn't he charged?"

"Because I made a mistake," Urban admitted. "I gave him the benefit of the doubt and assumed he would stick around. I had no idea he was about to go into hiding."

"I still can't believe he would kill an innocent woman," DC John Young chipped in. "Why would he do that?"

"We'll be looking into it," Urban said. "They're from the same city. Perhaps she knew things about him he didn't want getting out. We'll find out. Now, yesterday, another dead body was discovered in a wheelie bin over in Castel. We've yet to identify the dead woman but it is clear she has been dead for quite some time. At least three days judging by the state of decomposition. Pathology will give us a more exact TOD but we do have an initial forensic to go on. Rob."

DI Crown opened up a file in front of him. "The dead woman was wearing an expensive mohair jumper. The fibres on the jumper are as such that they are easily detachable. When I analysed a cross section of one of the fibres, I recognised something I'd seen before. I found similar fibres on a pair of trousers and a shirt taken from DI O'Reilly's apartment and when I compared the two, I got an exact match."

"How did O'Reilly manage to get mohair fibres on his clothes?" It was DCI Urban. "This isn't looking too good for him. Not good at all."

"None of this makes any sense," DC Young said. "It could be like you said and O'Reilly killed the Irishwoman, but two murders. Why would he kill the woman in the wheelie bin?"

"He's trying to blame a man he was instrumental in putting away fifteen years ago," Urban said. "Patrick Finney killed four women in Dublin at the turn of the century and O'Reilly was the one who caught him. It's all nonsense. Patrick Finney is nowhere near this island – the man escaped from jail last week and the last place he would come is Guernsey. O'Reilly is trying to make us believe Finney is out for revenge but I'm not buying it."

"What about the drawings on the bin lids?" DS Rowland asked. "The chalk pictures were Finney's calling cards. Why would O'Reilly copy them at the crime scenes?"
"Because he's trying to make it look like Finney is responsible of course. Have you not been listening?"
"I know O'Reilly," DS Rowland said. "He's a bit gruff but he's alright. He's not a murderer."
"That's enough, Carl," Urban glared at him. "This is exactly what I didn't want to happen. Just because O'Reilly is employed by the Island Police, it doesn't put him above the law."
"I didn't say it did, sir," DS Rowland said. "It's just that none of this makes any sense."
"Especially the first one," DC Young said. "Why would O'Reilly stick around after killing Mrs O'Connell? And why would he leave the murder weapon behind? He's a DI – he would know better than that."
"We're not here to understand why he did it, John, we're here to ascertain whether we have enough damning evidence to bring him in and charge him and as far as I'm concerned there is enough that ties him to the two murders to warrant just that. What we need to concentrate on now is finding the man. He's not at home and he wasn't at his girlfriend's house. Where else might he go?"

His question was met with silence.

"Somebody must have a suggestion," Urban said. "What do we know about the man?"
"He's a detective inspector." It was DC Young. "He's been here for about six months and in that time, he's cleared up every murder we've had."
"I've been considering that," Urban scratched his nose. "In the fifteen years I've been with the agency I can count the number of murders we've had on this island on the fingers of one hand. Then the Irishman appears and

suddenly people start dropping like flies. We've had around ten dead bodies since that man from Dublin arrived. Does anyone else think that's a bit odd?"

"Times have changed, sir." DS Henrietta Jones spoke for the first time. "I'm sure you'll find that homicides have increased all over."

"With respect, sir," DC Young said. "DI O'Reilly solved all of those murders – he didn't commit them."

"I'm getting tired of listening to this," Urban said. "We're not here for a meeting of the fucking O'Reilly fan club – we're here to investigate his involvement in two murders. I want you all to stop treating the man like a hero and go out there and find him. Find the fucking Irish bastard."

CHAPTER THIRTY

If O'Reilly had been a fly on the wall in the briefing room, he would have realised he had more support from the officers in the Border Agency than he could ever imagine. But he hadn't been a fly on the wall and right now he felt more isolated than ever before. He was well and truly on his own. In the past that was how he liked it – he'd never been much of a team player but right now he needed help. He needed the support of his team and he was well aware that none of them were in any position to offer it.

He crossed the road and scanned the street ahead of him. He was heading north on La Mont d'Aval in La Planque. The streets were quiet and there were very few people around. He walked through the gates into Saumarez Park and found a bench to sit on. A grey squirrel eyed him with suspicion then scuttled up into the branches of an old oak tree.

O'Reilly thought about a conversation he'd had not so long ago. He'd managed to get through to an old colleague. DS Ralph Randall was retired now but was still as sharp as ever. He'd been reluctant at first when O'Reilly told him what he wanted but, in the end, he'd given O'Reilly the contact details of an old source who in turn had agreed to get in touch with The Man. The phone call had come through an hour later.

The Man had many faces but his voice never changed. O'Reilly had flinched when he heard the soft baritone of the most feared criminal mind in Ireland.

"Smiley," he'd said. "I believe you're looking to discuss a bit of business."

This was the way he always spoke. Always paranoid, his words were carefully chosen so as not to give anything away.

"You could say that," O'Reilly told him.

"I'm always open to any new business opportunities."

O'Reilly told him everything. The Man listened to his every word without interrupting.

"That does sound like a bit of a quandary you're in there, Smiley," he said when O'Reilly had finished.

"I need your help," O'Reilly told him.

"I never liked Paddy Finney," The Man said. "Murder for murder's sake doesn't sit well with me."

"Can you help me or not?"

"What is it you're asking, Smiley?"

"He's set me up," O'Reilly said. "I want to turn that back around and lead the Island Police straight to him. But I can't do that on my own."

"I'll see what I can do."

O'Reilly decided to come out with it. "What do you want in return?" He was dreading asking it but he knew The Man's services didn't come cheap.

"Consider this a favour to an old friend, Smiley," The Man said.

You're no friend of mine, O'Reilly thought but he kept it to himself.

"But..." There was always a but with The Man. "I may need to come calling on you sometime in the future, so we'll leave it at that, shall we?"

O'Reilly knew there had to be a catch.

"How is this going to work?" he asked.

"I'll send someone," The Man said. "Someone you're going to like."

"I don't want that bastard from Belfast."

"I've stopped hiring from north of the border, Smiley," The Man said. "They're all far too political for my liking. No, you're going to like this one. She's a woman after my own heart."

"How do I contact her?"

"You don't," The Man said. "She'll get in touch with you. You'll know when she's arrived. Take care, Smiley."

That was when the line had gone dead. O'Reilly had checked the call history but the number The Man had phoned him on had been withheld. And now he knew there was nothing he could do but wait. Wait for whoever The Man was going to send to help him.

The squirrel appeared once more. Its eyes never leaving the downtrodden Irishman on the bench, it dared to come closer.

"I've got nothing for you, squirrel," O'Reilly said. "Bugger off."

The squirrel did just that. It cast one last glance at O'Reilly and darted off into the undergrowth.

O'Reilly stood up and started to walk towards the other end of the park. He had no idea where he was going – he just needed to feel like he was heading somewhere. He left through the northern exit and carried on walking along Rue Cohu. The Protestant Church looked closed but there was a van parked outside so O'Reilly walked up the steps to the entrance. He tried the door and found it to be open.

Two men were setting up some kind of stage at the back of the church. They were making such a din they didn't notice O'Reilly until he was only a few metres away.

The older of the two men looked up from his work. "Can I help you?"

"What are you doing?" O'Reilly asked him.

"We've got a string quartet playing tonight and tomorrow," the man replied. "We're just getting things set up."

"A string quartet?" O'Reilly repeated. "Sounds interesting."

"You should come along," the younger man said. "They're really cool. They play all sorts, from The Beatles to Metallica. It's really fresh music."

"I'll give it some thought."

"Are you alright, mate?" the older man asked. "You look a bit down."

"I've been worse," O'Reilly said. "I'll leave you to get on."

He turned to leave and was almost to the exit when he felt a hand on his shoulder. He braced himself for an attack but when he turned around, he realised it was the younger man. He was holding something in his hands.
"Take these," he said and held out two tickets. "I shouldn't be giving these out but you look like you need cheering up."
O'Reilly didn't know what to say. He looked at the tickets and hesitated before accepting them.
"They're valid for tonight's gig," the young man said. "Bring a friend – I promise that you'll enjoy it."
"Thank you," O'Reilly said. "Thank you very much."

He carried on walking up to Green Forest and realised he'd never been to this part of the island. Guernsey was small but there was more of it to explore than he thought. He spotted a Police car further up the road and managed to get inside a flower shop just in time. He looked out of the window and saw it drive past slowly. He wondered if it was out looking for him.
I'm a man on the run, he thought. *Yesterday I was a DI just doing my job and now I'm on the run from the Police.*

The more he thought about it, the more absurd it seemed. His colleagues were hunting him down. He'd gone from hunter to hunted in the blink of an eye.

He dared to go outside and carried on walking. He needed a place to hide – somewhere they wouldn't think to look, but he didn't have a clue where that place was. In the end he decided he would find the nearest hotel or B&B, check in and stay there until he could think of something better. He was certain that Franklin Urban was making use of all the resources at his disposal to hunt him down and walking aimlessly around the island wasn't a particularly good idea. The arrogant head of the Border Agency wouldn't stop until O'Reilly was found, and O'Reilly was damned if he was going to make Urban's job easy.

CHAPTER THIRTY ONE

"This isn't right, Ma'am," DC Owen said to Superintendent Anne Hayes.
DC Owen had decided enough was enough and gone to see the Superintendent to see if she could do something about the way O'Reilly was being treated.
"My hands are tied, Katie," Hayes said. "DCI Urban has the investigation and there's nothing I can do about it."
"But DI O'Reilly has been treated like a common criminal, Ma'am. Urban is using this as an excuse to carry out his own personal vendetta. You know how he feels about the DI. O'Reilly made a fool out of him when he first came here and Urban is just exacting his revenge."
"My hands are tied," Superintendent Hayes said again. "The evidence against DI O'Reilly is quite damning and he isn't doing himself any favours by disappearing into thin air."
"He doesn't have much of a choice, Ma'am," DC Owen insisted. "Urban is going to arrest him, and the DI knows that'll mean he won't be able to catch this Patrick Finney monster."
"We don't know for certain Patrick Finney is behind these murders, Katie," Superintendent Hayes said. "There's nothing to link him to either victim."
"That's because he's done everything he can to make it look like O'Reilly was responsible. We should be putting all out efforts into finding Finney – not harassing one of the best detectives on this island."

"My hands are tied," Superintendent Hayes said for the third time. "If DI O'Reilly hadn't gone into hiding, we would be able to sort this mess out but as things stand, he's only succeeded in making DCI Urban even more suspicious. It's the Border Agency's party and there's nothing you or I can do about it."
DC Owen shook her head and stood up. "It's just not right."

"Katie," Superintendent Hayes said when DC Owen had reached the door. "If Liam gets in touch with you, you need to inform DCI Urban. Is that understood?"
"Of course, Ma'am," DC Owen lied. "But I very much doubt he would risk contacting someone from the station."
"Liam needs to hand himself in," Superintendent Hayes added. "It's for the best."

DC Owen returned to her office, made some coffee and sat down in front of her laptop. She wanted to help O'Reilly but she wasn't sure where to start. She knew for a fact he had no involvement in the two recent murders, but if it was as he said and Patrick Finney was responsible, she needed to come up with a plan to find the Irish serial killer.

She typed his name into the search bar and was astonished by what she saw on the screen. There were scores and scores of results for the notorious psychopath. She clicked on the first one and started reading. It was an article from the Irish Times and it was dated almost exactly fifteen years ago. The piece had been written shortly after Finney had received his sentence – life without the possibility of parole and it went into detail about the despicable things the man had done.

His first victim was killed on the 14th of June. Under the light of the full moon Kathy Wilson was slaughtered in her bathroom. Kathy was a second-year student at Dublin University and she was alone in the house when Finney killed her. It was the holidays – her housemates had all gone home for the summer but Kathy had stayed in Dublin to earn some money working in a restaurant. It was unclear as to how Finney gained access to Kathy's house but the Times speculated, he probably used some kind of ruse to get inside. Finney was a natural charmer and ladies' man and he probably used his charisma to get inside Kathy's house.

DC Owen flinched when she read what Kathy Wilson had been subjected to. She was found in the bath tub with her neck sliced open so deeply it had almost been detached from her body. The Special Detective Unit of the Garda found nothing at the scene to give them any idea where to start looking. There were no fingerprints or hair samples besides the dead woman's and after conducting numerous meticulous searches it transpired that Finney left behind no physical evidence whatsoever. What he did leave behind, however was a crude chalk drawing on the mirror in the bathroom. The stick drawing of the woman and the snake had everyone working on the case baffled. Nobody could figure out what it meant.

DC Owen spotted O'Reilly's name further down the page. He was quoted as saying the Special Detective Unit were working on a number of leads and were confident that the monster who did this to Miss Wilson would be caught soon.

He wasn't and Finney killed again a month later. On July 13th Lisa Mulligan was found by her husband with her throat cut. Mr Mulligan had returned home from work to find his wife in the kitchen. Once again O'Reilly and his team found nothing but the chalk drawing at the scene. Nobody in the neighbouring houses had noticed anything suspicious and no forensic evidence was found.

DC Owen sipped her coffee and carried on reading. Finney claimed his third victim on the 12th of August. Once again, the moon was full and once again the detectives called to the scene came up with nothing to point them in any firm direction. The city of Dublin was held in the grip of terror. Women were afraid to go out under the light of the full moon and it seemed like this monster would never be caught.

A month later the team in the Special Detective Unit got a breakthrough but it came with a huge price tag. DC Ellie Finch was one of the detectives on O'Reilly's team and Finney made his first mistake by killing her. DC Owen knew the details and she also knew that DC Finch was Finney's final victim. A black and white photograph of a younger O'Reilly was shown further down the page. Beneath it he was quoted as saying it was through dogged determination and perseverance that his team finally apprehended Patrick Finney and he was confident that the worst serial killer in Irish history would receive the harshest punishment possible.

DC Owen could feel the anger starting to boil up inside her. O'Reilly was the man who'd brought this monster down and now he was the one being treated like a monster. It was all wrong and she needed to try and do something about it. She scrolled down the page and found herself staring into the eyes of Patrick Duncan Finney. She had to admit he really was very attractive. With his tanned skin and blue eyes, she could see how women would be taken in by him. And he really didn't look like a depraved monster. He looked more like a film star than a serial killer.

Even though she knew Finney could have changed considerably after fifteen years behind bars DC Owen downloaded the photograph and printed a copy for herself. She glanced at it once more, folded it up and put it in her pocket.

CHAPTER THIRTY TWO

O'Reilly opened the door to his room and went inside. He'd found a modest, family-run B&B in Les Rouvets and checked in using a false name. He paid in cash and the sleepy-eyed receptionist hadn't asked him for any ID. He'd exhausted half of his remaining cash to pay for three days and he knew he wouldn't be able to withdraw any more. It would be far too risky to use an ATM – Urban would probably be monitoring that.

He hoped the three days he'd booked would be enough time to stay hidden. He also hoped that help from The Man would arrive soon. The faceless phantom had mentioned something about sending a woman and O'Reilly wondered if there was a reason for this. He would find out soon enough.

He dumped his coat on the only chair in the room and looked around. The room was situated at the back of the building and the view from the window was far from spectacular. The room looked out onto the back of a double storey place that was badly in need of a lick of paint.

O'Reilly sat on the bed and for the first time since the start of this whole fiasco he had some time to process everything that had happened. The discovery of Delores O'Connell's lifeless body seemed like it had happened weeks ago even though it had only been thirty-six hours since he'd stumbled across her outside the Butchers.

O'Reilly closed his eyes and tried to piece together the chain of events like he would in any normal murder investigation. It had all started two days earlier when the brick was thrown through his window and he ought to have known right then that Patrick Finney was initiating a sinister and clever plan. Then there had been the faceless driver of the black car. O'Reilly was positive it had been Finney following him in the Yaris.

He was certain now that there was something about Delores O'Connell's visit to the station on Monday morning that was connected. She wasn't there to report a crime – somehow that was part of Finney's plan too. And when she turned up in the Red Snapper at the same time as O'Reilly surely that had to be more than coincidence. Shortly after that she was killed and O'Reilly was the one to find her body.

He then remembered the mysterious package he'd been sent but he still didn't understand the significance of that package. He wasn't aware of the dead woman in the wheelie bin nor was he aware that fibres from the woman's mohair jumper had exploded out of that package and covered his clothes with enough evidence to give Franklin Urban and the Border Agency enough cause to seek him out.

O'Reilly's thoughts turned once more to Delores O'Connell. Something about the whole thing was niggling him. Their paths had crossed at some time or other back in Dublin but O'Reilly couldn't remember anything specific and he was still unable to work out what role she'd played in Patrick Finney's mission to exact revenge.

He looked at the phone on the table next to the bed. There were no numbers stored in the phone and he couldn't remember any of his contacts' details off the top of his head.

"Technology is a pile of shite," he cursed to himself.

The modern world had created a society that relied far too much on the machines they now took for granted. In the blink of an eye all that information could be wiped out. Nobody committed phone numbers to memory anymore – they left that up to the devices they carried around with them.

O'Reilly needed to find out something important but he had no idea how he was going to get hold of that information. He swiped his phone and opened up Google. He searched for the hospital where Dr Guthrie Lille headed up the Pathology department and found a list of numbers. As he'd expected they were all landline numbers. He dialled the first one and got through to the reception desk at the hospital.

"I'm trying to get hold of Dr Lille," he told the man. "But I've misplaced his number. Could you please tell me his mobile number?"

O'Reilly half-expected what came next.

"I'm sorry, sir," the man said. "But I'm not allowed to give out that kind of information. I can put you through to the Pathology department."

"Can you do that, then?"

He waited a few seconds before a woman asked him. "Pathology. How can I help you?"

"I need to speak to Dr Lille," O'Reilly told her. "It's rather urgent."

"Dr Lille is in a meeting right now," the woman informed him. "Can I help you with anything?"

O'Reilly didn't know what to say to her.

"I'll try again later," he managed and rang off.

He got off the bed and started to pace around the room. He decided to weigh up his options. He could call Assumpta but he wasn't sure if his daughter's phone was being monitored by Urban and his team. He found the details of the Gazette and called the number on the website.

"Guernsey Gazette."

It was Assumpta's colleague Keith.

"Could I speak to Assumpta O'Reilly, please?" O'Reilly asked him.

There was no switchboard at the Gazette and Keith's attempt to muffle the phone by placing his hand over the handset failed miserably.

"Assumpta," O'Reilly heard him shout. "It's for you."

"Assumpta O'Reilly," she came on the line shortly afterwards.

"Summi," O'Reilly said. "Don't say anything. Are you somewhere we can talk without being overheard?"

"Hold on."

The line went dead and O'Reilly wondered if they'd been cut off.

"Where are you, Dad?" Assumpta asked after a few seconds.

"Some B&B," O'Reilly replied rather vaguely. "That's not important. I need you to do something for me."

"Urban is all over me," she told him. "They're watching me like a hawk and they're not even trying to hide it. This is serious, Dad."

"Listen to me," O'Reilly said. "There's something not quite right about how Delores O'Connell was killed. It all seems too well-planned if that makes any sense."

"Nothing makes any sense right now."

"Guthrie will have conducted the post mortem by now," O'Reilly said. "I need to know what he found."

"What for?"

"Because I have a feeling Delores and Finney were in this together."

"You're talking nonsense now, Dad," Assumpta said. "How can two people plot a murder when one of them is the victim?'

"I don't know, but that's what it looks like to me. Please, Summi, get hold of Guthrie at the hospital and see if he found anything unusual."

"Are you going to be alright, Dad?" Assumpta asked.

"I don't know, Summi," he said. "I really don't' know."

"Did you hear about the other murder?"

"The one over in Castel?"

"That's it."

"Katie just told me they found another chalk drawing. She didn't go into too much detail apart from that."

"A woman was found dead in a wheelie bin over in Castel. The details haven't been released but you know how tongues wag on this island. And I'm afraid the Herald know about you going into hiding."

"How the hell did that get out?"

"Two guesses."

"Eric Rivers?" O'Reilly said.

"Rivers somehow got word about the chalk drawings and the fact that you're a suspect. I don't know how he found out but the Herald have already stuck something up on their online forum."

"It was Finney," O'Reilly said. "This is something Finney would do. He's back, Summi and it appears he's worse than before. He wants revenge and he's going to stop at nothing to get it. See what you can find out from Dr Lille. Delores O'Connell was a part of all this, you mark my words."

CHAPTER THIRTY THREE

"Cancer?" DCI Urban said.

His team had gathered in the briefing room for a case meeting. DS Rowland had the Pathology report for Delores O'Connell on the screen of the laptop in front of him.

"Stage 4 lung cancer, sir," Rowland elaborated. "Dr Lille managed to contact Mrs O'Connell's specialist in Dublin. The cancer had reached the chronic metastatic stage and spread beyond control. The woman was barely alive."

"What does this mean?" DC Young asked.

"It means whoever killed her put her out of her misery," DS Rowland said. "If you'll excuse me for sounding rather cruel. The poor woman was looking at perhaps two weeks if she was lucky."

"So, she was dying," DCI Urban said. "It doesn't alter the fact that she was murdered. And we need to disregard the cancer and concentrate all our efforts on catching the man responsible. DI O'Reilly appears to have vanished into thin air. We've checked all of his usual haunts and he is nowhere to be seen. I've put an all points out and every police officer on this island is on the lookout for him. He can't have gone far, so I'm confident we'll have him in custody before the end of the day. Now, before we continue, I've scheduled a press conference for six this evening. I believe we'll increase our chances of finding O'Reilly if we have more pairs of eyes out there looking for him."

"Do you think that's such a good idea, sir?" DC Young asked. "You know what the press can be like – this is going to be like feeding DI O'Reilly to the lions when we don't actually know for sure he was involved in any of this."

DCI Urban didn't reply to this. He didn't have to. The expression on his face told DC Young exactly what he thought of the young DC's comment. Urban looked absolutely furious.

"He's got a point, sir," DS Jones said. "With respect, I don't think a press conference right now is going to do anyone any favours. Speculation will be rife and it could be detrimental to the investigation once the press get wind of what's been happening."

"Do I have to remind you of the evidence we have against O'Reilly?" Urban said. "What is it about that Irish bastard that you all have to defend the man? He was found at the scene with the murder weapon in his hand – fibres from the jumper the second victim was wearing were found on his clothing and now the man has gone into hiding. Can you tell me honestly that if it were some other Joe Soap suspected of these murders you would be so against a press conference? No, I don't think you would. Now, can we try not to let our judgment be clouded and continue with this briefing in a professional manner?"

Nobody spoke for a while. DCI Urban's little tirade had silenced his team for the time being.

"Our main priority right now is finding O'Reilly," Urban said after a while. "We'll be keeping an eye on those closest to him. His daughter and girlfriend are being monitored as are some of the members of his team."

"Do you think they'll try and help him?" DS Rowland asked. "His team, I mean?"

"I do, yes. That man seems to have a knack of commanding a bizarre kind of loyalty and I'm concerned about certain detectives compromising my investigation. I assure you I will not allow that to happen and should I find out it is happening I will not hesitate to come down hard on those responsible. Now, can we press on? Rob?"

"Besides the fibres from the mohair jumper, we have very little to go on, sir," The Border Agency forensics officer said. "There was very little blood in and around the wheelie bin so it's safe to assume she was killed somewhere else and dumped in the bin much later. I've analysed the chalk drawing and

I can confirm it was drawn by the same hand as the one found at the scene of the Delores O'Connell murder."

"But we already knew that, didn't we?" DCI Urban said.

"I've sent photographs off to an expert, sir. Something about the drawings struck me as odd and I want to have my suspicions confirmed by someone more qualified than me."

"What was odd about the drawings?" DC Young said.

"I'll show you."

DI Crown stood up and turned on the big screen at the back of the room. He flipped open his laptop and brought up the photographs he'd taken of the chalk drawings.

"This is the one found on the lid of the bin down the road from where Delores O'Connell was killed. Some of it has faded in places but you can still make out what it's supposed to depict."

"A stick woman with a snake round her neck," DS Jones said.

"And the number at the bottom is significant," DI Crown said. "The number is supposed to tell us Mrs O'Connell is the sixth victim. There was a number five on the drawing on the lid of the bin the latest victim was found in."

"Which also means Delores O'Connell was killed after the woman in the bin," DC Young pointed out. "Even though her body was discovered first. What does that mean?"

"It means that DI O'Reilly wanted to confuse things," DCI Urban said. "Is there a point to this, DI Crown or are we about to get into another debate about the virtues of that damn Irishman?"

DI Crown brought up the photograph of the other chalk drawing.

"This is the one found over in Castel. If I place them next to each other you'll see they're almost identical. They were drawn by the same hand."

"Where are you going with this, Rob?" DCI Urban made a point of looking at his watch.

"I'll show you, sir." DI Crown approached the screen and took out a marker pen. "If I go over the outline of the drawings I can't quite stick to the lines. I'm no artist but tracing a picture shouldn't be that hard, but here it's tricky because the flow of the chalk drawing is opposite of what my brain is telling me is natural."

"I'm not following you, sir." It was DC Young.

"Take the woman's head, for example. You'll see there's a swirl at the bottom left-hand corner. It's barely visible but it's there. On my effort the swirl is at the top on the right."

"What exactly does that mean?" DS Jones asked.

"Like I say I need to get it confirmed," DI Crown said and sat back down. "But if I'm not mistaken whoever did these chalk drawings was left-handed."

CHAPTER THIRTY FOUR

O'Reilly had dozed off and he didn't know where he was for a second when he opened his eyes. Something had woken him – it was a strange sound coming from outside the door of his room. It sounded like someone was trying to get inside. He got up off the bed and walked quietly over to the door. The scraping sound stopped. O'Reilly pressed his ear to the wall but he couldn't hear anything outside in the corridor. After listening for another minute or so he decided he must have been mistaken. It was probably one of the other guests returning to their room.

He looked at the tickets on the table and sighed. Victoria would have enjoyed watching a string quartet in a church but that wasn't going to happen now. He turned on the tiny kettle to make some tea and went to the bathroom to splash some water on his face. It was not yet dark outside but the sun was going down. He towelled himself dry and went to make the tea.

A woman was standing next to the bed. She was tall and slim and when she turned to look at him O'Reilly reckoned her to be in her mid-thirties. Her black hair was tied back in a tight bun and her eyes never left his. He didn't know what to do – he just found himself staring at her. She raised a hand to her lips and placed a finger over her lips to indicate she wanted him to keep quiet.

"Does anyone else know where you are?"

That was it. There were no introductions, no explanation as to why she was standing in his room, nothing.

O'Reilly found himself shaking his head.

"This is how it's going to work."

Her accent was hard to place. There was a hint of Dublin in there but it was subtle and O'Reilly guessed she'd been away from Ireland for quite some time.

"You are not to contact anyone," she continued. "Nobody. You don't leave this room and you do exactly as I say. Is that understood, Liam? Is it alright if I call you Liam?"

"It's my name," O'Reilly said. "And since you know my name it's only fair you offer me yours in return."

"Cara. And that's all I'm going to tell you about me."

"How did you find me?" O'Reilly asked.

She nodded to the mobile phone on the bedside table.

"That's impossible," O'Reilly said. "It's a prepaid and it's not even registered on the network."

"There are ways, Liam. It's complicated but let's just say when The Man phoned you, he found a way inside the phone."

O'Reilly's detective brain couldn't just leave it at that. He was used to phone taps and tracking using cell towers but there was no way he could be tracked down to a room in a B&B via his mobile phone.

"There is no way that can be done, Cara."

"Not all technology is accessible to everyone, Liam," she said. "The Police included. When The Man phoned you, he got inside your phone. You used your WiFi earlier and that activated your Assisted GPS. In the old days the location was wider but I use a program that can pinpoint your location to as little as three square metres."

O'Reilly was finding all of this hard to take in. "Are you telling me you can know where I am at all times? You can tell when I'm having a piss?"

"If you're in the habit of taking your phone with you to the bathroom, yes."

"So, Finney could also make use of this technology?"

She shook her head. "Patrick Finney is out of touch. He's been out of circulation for far too long. He's old school – he uses old school methods and that's what we're going to use to our advantage. Are you hungry?"

"What?"

"You must be hungry. You haven't left this room in hours. I can pick us up something to eat. I just need to make sure everything is secure then I'll get some takeaway. Do you have any preferences?"

O'Reilly wasn't sure why but he started to laugh. This whole situation was so utterly surreal he was actually finding it amusing. He felt like he'd been thrown into the middle of a spy film. He half expected a TV team to burst into the room any second and tell him he'd been the victim of a prank.

"I could eat some fish and chips," he said. "No vinegar though."

"I'll see what I can do," Cara said. "We need to talk about how this is going to pan out."

She walked over to the window and peeked through a gap in the curtains. Then she left the room without saying anything else. O'Reilly made his tea and sat back down on the bed. He was in trouble - he was in serious trouble. He was being hunted by the Police and he was being hunted by a serial killer hell bent on exacting revenge. His fate was in the hands of an underworld crime boss and for the first time ever he felt like he'd lost all control of his life. The Man had made good on his offer of help but O'Reilly still wasn't sure if he could trust that help or not. For all he knew Finney, the Man and the woman who called herself Cara could be in it together. Nothing would surprise him considering everything that had happened. A ridiculous thought occurred to him. He decided he would leave it up to the toss of a coin. But this coin was in the shape of a takeaway fish and chips. If Cara brought back crap fish and chips, he would turn himself in and put himself in the hands of Franklin Urban and the Border Agency.

His mind was made up an hour later. He scrunched up the newspaper and wiped his mouth with a napkin.

"That was grand."

"That's quite an appetite you've got there," Cara said.

O'Reilly had polished off his fish supper and half of hers.

He threw the newspaper in the rubbish bin. "You were going to tell me how this was going to pan out. Do I need to be worried?"

"Not if you do exactly what I say," Cara said. "You might want to open one of those beers I brought before I start talking."

"Later," O'Reilly said. "How are you going to help me out here?"

"I need to wash my hands."

She came out of the bathroom and pulled the chair closer to the bed. "This is going to take a bit of time."

"I don't have time," O'Reilly said. "I've got hardly any money and I'm still in the same clothes I was wearing last night. The entire Island Police is out looking for me and it's only a matter of time before they track me down."

"They won't," Cara said. "I'll divert them. What we need to concentrate on now is Finney."

"Do you know him?"

"I know of him. If he's on this island he'll be easy to find."

"He is on this island," O'Reilly said. "He's out for revenge."

"Then we'll use that against him. Try not to take this personally."

"How the feck can I not take this personally? The man is busy ruining my life. I take that kind of thing extremely personally."

"Don't. Tell me everything he's done so far."

O'Reilly told her. He related the chain of events from when the brick came flying through his window up until he was forced to go into hiding."

"And this Border Agency?" Cara said when he'd finished. "Are they really so incompetent?"

"Worse," O'Reilly said. "But the bodach in charge, DCI Franklin Urban has a beef with me. I made him look like an idiot when I first came here and he hasn't forgotten about it. Finney isn't the only one out for revenge here – Urban is second in line. Finney has given him me on a plate and Urban is so blinkered he can't see how convenient all of this so-called evidence against me is. The man isn't even concerned about my reasoning. He's probably not even looking into motive."

"Let's not get side-tracked," Cara said. "Urban isn't a problem. Finney is. But I've come up against bigger problems than him before."

"He must have friends," O'Reilly said. "There's no way he could have managed to stage an escape from Portlaoise without a lot of help."

"That part is obvious."

"And he must have had help getting here to the island. It's clear he still has friends on the outside."

"The trouble with friends," Cara said. "Is very few of them are really friends. Patrick Finney has people but The Man has more people. I'll be in touch. Don't leave this room."

"Am I going to regret this?" O'Reilly asked her when she was standing by the door.

"No," Cara said without turning round. "You're not."

CHAPTER THIRTY FIVE

"We've got a location, sir," DS Carl Rowland said to DCI Urban. "O'Reilly's service provider has given us a rough location. They've managed to pinpoint it to a couple of hundred square metres."

"The press conference is due to start in thirty minutes," Urban reminded him. "It is imperative I head up that conference. What's the location?"

"That's the interesting thing, sir," Rowland said. "They traced his phone to Vazon. It's where his girlfriend lives. I think he's hiding out at his girlfriend's place again."

"Get over there. Get over there and arrest the man. Kick the door in if you have to. I have to get ready for the press conference. The cars streaming in outside suggest this is going to be one of the most high-profile cases we've ever had on this island and I'm going to make sure the Border Agency get every bit of credit due to them. You and DC Young can go and pick up the Irishman and I'll try and keep the press happy until you get back. This is perfect timing, Carl. If we can have DI O'Reilly in custody before the end of the press conference the timing couldn't be more perfect. I'd better get in there. I'm going to be remembered for this – I can sense it."

Urban walked inside the conference room with his head held high. Flanked by DS Henrietta Jones and DI Rob Crown he looked like a man on the verge of something spectacular. DI Crown had been reluctant when Urban had asked him to sit in – the Head of Forensics in the Border Agency preferred to work behind the scenes and the limelight wasn't for him, but Urban had insisted. He wanted Crown there by his side to offer the press contingency a taster of the forensic evidence against O'Reilly straight from the horse's mouth.

Crown's reluctance wasn't only because of his dislike of the limelight – the forensics officer was still troubled about the chalk drawings. He was convinced they had been drawn by a left-handed person but Urban had dismissed his theory, claiming it wasn't important. Plus, Crown had done some digging after the briefing and what he'd found out was rather disturbing. DI O'Reilly was right-handed, there was no doubt about that. But Patrick Finney wasn't. Ireland's most notorious serial killer was left-handed and the more DI Crown pondered on the subject the more convinced he was O'Reilly was telling the truth. Patrick Finney was on the island, and he was out for revenge.

The noise inside the conference room died down when DCI Urban tapped the microphone on the table in front of him. The loud chattering and scraping of chairs subsided as the press contingency waited to hear what the arrogant Head of the Border Agency had to say.

Urban smiled at DS Henrietta Jones. "I've got a good feeling about this, Henrietta."

He turned his attention to the crowd of people in front of him. One of the journalists in the front row was Assumpta O'Reilly. She was discussing something with Fiona, the editor of the Guernsey Gazette. Urban looked away when she looked up at him.

"Sorry to keep you all waiting," he said even though it was six on the dot. "Thank you all for coming. My name is Franklin Urban and I'm in charge of the Border Agency here on the island. That's Franklin as in the Roosevelt spelling of the name. I'll ask you to keep any questions to the end and to please bear with me – there is a lot to go through. I'm of the opinion that the Police and the press need to work with one another and total transparency is required, so I will not leave anything out. Let's make a start, shall we?"

* * *

DS Rowland and DC Young parked outside Victoria Radcliffe's house just as DCI Urban was opening up the press conference. O'Reilly's service provider had informed them that two base stations had picked up the signal from his sim card and they'd narrowed the area down to Vazon beach in the west to the golf course further east. Victoria Radcliffe's house was almost smack bang in the middle of the location Urban's team had been given.

"Do you think he's here?" DC Young asked.

"His sim is somewhere in the three hundred metre radius the cell company gave us," DS Rowland said. "But I'd be very surprised if he went back to his girlfriend's place. O'Reilly isn't stupid and he knows we'd keep coming back here."

"The first thing I'd do is dump my sim card," DC Young added. "Get rid of it. Even if the phone is switched off the sim can still be traced. Perhaps O'Reilly didn't know that."

"Let's go and see if he's here, shall we?"

They got out of the car and walked up the path towards the house. A white van with the Radcliffe Bikes logo was parked outside.

"This is a really nice place," DC Young said. "I'd love to live in a house. I'm getting tired of all the rules and regulations in my apartment complex."

"You won't be able to afford a place like this on what the Island Police pay you, John. It looks like there's somebody home – the lights are on inside."

Victoria Radcliffe seemed surprised to see them. She looked the two Border Agency detectives up and down.

"Can I help you?"

DS Rowland showed her his ID. "DS Rowland and this is DC Young. Can we come inside please?"

"Be my guest," Victoria said and stepped aside. "What's this all about?"

"Is DI O'Reilly here?" Rowland asked.

"No."

"Are you sure?" DC Young said.

"Of course I'm sure."

"When was the last time you saw DI O'Reilly?" Rowland said.

"Early this morning. He left here about six and I haven't seen him since."

A large white cat appeared down the hallway. The rather obese animal looked up at them and disappeared inside a room to the left.

"Has DI O'Reilly been in touch with you at all today?" DC Young said.

"I told you," Victoria said. "He left in quite a hurry this morning and that was the last time I heard from him. He didn't kill that woman. You know that, don't you?"

"I'm afraid we can't discuss that," DS Rowland said. "Would you mind if we had a look around?"

"Do I have a choice?"

"Yes, you do, but it would be better for all of us if you cooperated. We could come back with a warrant, but if you say O'Reilly isn't here there's no harm in us having a look, is there?"

Victoria shrugged her shoulders. "Be my guest. You won't find anything."

Rowland and Young reappeared fifteen minutes later.

"Sorry for the inconvenience," DC Young said. "But we had to check."

"Can you leave me in peace now?" Victoria said.

"I don't see why not," DS Rowland told her. "If DI O'Reilly does get in contact with you, please give us a call. He's doing himself no favours by hiding away like this."

"I'll bear that in mind."

"Just one more question," DC Young said.

DS Rowland frowned at him.

"What on earth do you feed that cat?" DC Young asked. "That is the biggest moggy I've ever seen."

"She has a thyroid problem," Victoria said. "Could you please leave now?"

CHAPTER THIRTY SIX

"On Monday evening, the body of a woman was found outside a Butchers shop here in St Peter Port," DCI Urban told the crowd of journalists. "Her throat had been cut and we believe she died instantly. Witnesses who arrived on the scene say they saw a man standing next to her dead body. He was acting strangely, and he was covered in the woman's blood. This very same man was seen engaging in an altercation earlier that same evening – an altercation that ended up with the dead woman being thrown to the floor. To put another perspective on the matter, we've recently learned the identity of the dead woman. Her name is Delores O'Connell, she's an Irish national and she was sixty-three years old."

He stopped there to let this information sink in.

"Mrs O'Connell had also been diagnosed with terminal cancer. We spoke to her doctors back in Ireland and it transpires she didn't have long left. Why she was brutally murdered remains a mystery, but we have gathered important evidence, both physical and forensic and we are positive we will bring Mrs O'Connell's murderer in within the next forty-eight hours. We have a suspect in mind, and it is only a matter of time before he is apprehended."

Urban glanced across at Assumpta but her facial expression gave nothing away.

"Yesterday afternoon," he continued. "The body of an as yet unidentified woman was discovered in a wheelie bin in Castel. This woman also had her throat cut. A man matching the description of the man seen standing next to Delores O'Connell was spotted close to where the wheelie bin was and we now have irrefutable proof that this man came into contact with the victim."

A woman in the second row put up her hand.

"I will answer any questions at the end," DCI Urban told her. "There must be a few of you who are wondering why the Border Agency has been tasked with the job of investigating two murders on the island. You're probably thinking this kind of crime is not within our usual scope of expertise and I'm going to tell you exactly why that is."

DS Jones looked at him with an expression of shock on her face. DI Crown tapped him on the shoulder and shook his head.

The room was abuzz with expectation. The woman in the second row raised her hand again but Urban ignored her. He waited for the low murmuring to increase in volume then he tapped the microphone to indicate he was going to give them something.

"Sir," DI Crown whispered in Urban's ear. "This isn't a good idea."

"It's a brilliant idea, Rob," Urban said. "They came here for a story, and I'm going to give them the story of a lifetime."

"O'Reilly will be skinned alive, sir," DS Jones added.

"Could we have a bit of hush, please," Urban spoke into the microphone. "The Border Agency has taken on the investigation because the detectives in the Murder Squad were faced with a conflict of interest."

The noise inside the room increased once more.

"We have irrefutable evidence that one of the detectives in that team was involved in both murders. It saddens me to have to be the bearer of these dire tidings. It sickens me to the very core have to be the harbinger of such bad news but I feel it is my duty to give you the truth."

"Get on with it," a man's voice was heard from the back.

Urban couldn't tell where the voice came from.

"The suspect in question was seen shortly after Mrs O'Connell was killed," Urban continued. "His prints were found on the murder weapon and his clothes were covered in her blood. Fibres from an item of clothing worn by the second victim were also found when we carried out a search of his residence."

"Stop wanking to the sound of your own voice," a woman shouted. "And get on with it."

DS Jones gasped.

"The suspect has gone into hiding," Urban carried on regardless. "And that's why I need your help this evening. Our number one suspect in the brutal murders of two women is Detective Inspector Liam O'Reilly."

The whole room erupted. Voices were raised and questions were fired at the Head of the Border Agency from every direction.

"You're a fecking idiot."

Urban flinched. He didn't realise Assumpta O'Reilly had such a loud voice. DI Rob Crown got to his feet. The forensics officer had clearly had enough. He made his way towards the door at the back of the room without saying anything else to DCI Urban.

Urban took a few deep breaths to compose himself.

"Any questions?"

The din in the room got even louder.

"Can we have a bit of order?" Urban said. "One at a time please."

"Where is O'Reilly now?" a man sitting behind Assumpta asked.

It was Fred Viking, or Fred the Ed as he was known in journalistic circles.

"We're working round the clock to find him," Urban said.

"Why was O'Reilly allowed to escape?" a woman standing in the wings asked. "If you found all this evidence, how was he allowed to escape? Are you telling us you let him go because he's a policeman?"

"It's not like that at all. DI O'Reilly was given the benefit of the doubt, that's all. He was advised to stay in contact but he chose to disregard that advice."

"Why would a respected DI leave so much evidence behind for you to find?"

It was Assumpta's boss, Fiona. The room fell silent when her question was posed. The editor of the Gazette had raised a valid point.

"Surely an experienced detective wouldn't be so stupid as to hand you so much evidence on a plate," Fiona added. "How can you explain that?"

Urban couldn't explain it. More than one member of his team had brought up this exact point and he'd chosen to ignore it.

"Well?" Fiona urged.

"Everybody makes mistakes," Urban offered. "We're all only human, DI O'Reilly included."

"Do you honestly expect us to believe a man like DI O'Reilly would kill two women?" Eric Rivers said. "This is the most ridiculous thing I've ever heard."

"It is what it is," Urban said.

"It's the biggest pile of shite that's ever spilled from your mouth," Assumpta joined in. "You've had it in for DI O'Reilly ever since he made you look like a prick when he first arrived."

"Nobody has made me look like a prick."

"No," Rivers shouted. "You don't need much help in that department. Is there anything else you'd like to share with us? Perhaps the Chief Officer is a closet cross dresser."

The whole room erupted. Urban looked to DS Jones for support but she looked like she wanted the earth to swallow her up.

"I think you have enough to go on for the time being," Urban said. "As I said earlier, I would like to ask the public for their help in finding DI O'Reilly. We have prepared a press release and I would strongly advise every one of you to take what I have said seriously. This is no joke; I can promise you that."

He stood up and walked through the same door DI Crown had exited a few minutes earlier. Crown was standing by the coffee machine in the corner. He heard Urban coming and turned around.

"You left me in the lurch back there," the DCI said. "Don't do that again."

"With respect, sir," DI Crown took the beaker from the machine. "You made us look like incompetent idiots."

"Excuse me?"

"You made a laughing stock out of the Border Agency, and none of the people inside that room took any of what you said seriously. And to be brutally honest, I don't blame them. This whole O'Reilly thing is a farce."

"Do I have to remind you who you're talking to?"

"No, sir," Crown said. "You made it very clear back there who was doing the talking. This is going to end badly, you mark my words."

"What the hell is that supposed to mean?"

"What I said. It's going to end badly. Heads are going to roll and if top brass have any wits about them, they'll start rolling heads from the top down. I'm off home."

He threw the half-full beaker in the bin and left a wide-mouthed DCI Urban in his wake.

CHAPTER THIRTY SEVEN

Patrick Finney was observing. He was watching the woman in the second-floor apartment in Vazon again. He'd been watching her for quite some time now but still she'd shown no indication of leaving. The apartment complex was very secure. There was a guard manning the gate at the entrance and there was no way Finney would be able to scale the twelve-foot-high wall. He was nowhere near as agile as he once was.

No, he was going to have to wait. Wait for the woman to come to him. Waiting was no problem to Patrick Finney – he'd spent a third of his life waiting and he'd learned how to become very good at it. When he was locked up in Portlaoise he'd passed the time by imagining all those who'd come before him. The sick, the twisted and the notorious had all shared the same space and Patrick Finney had found this quite comforting. There was a history within the walls of Portlaoise that was still alive in the bricks and mortar.

The lights had gone off inside the second-floor apartment – the woman was coming to him.

Unbeknown to Finney, someone was observing him. He couldn't see her from her hiding place in the car down the street, but she was watching his every movement.

The door to the woman's apartment opened, she locked it and made her way down the single flight of stairs. Finney shifted his position so he could see where she was going and watched as she set off on foot towards the boom gate. She spoke a few words to the security guard, turned left and walked purposefully in the direction of Vazon town.

Cara Kenny locked her car and set off in the direction Finney had gone. The monster from Dublin had no idea he was being followed – he was too focused on his own prey, and Cara found it easy to stay a safe distance behind, undetected. The bizarre procession of three continued for another few minutes then the woman from the apartment complex stopped at a bus stop. She was planning on taking a bus somewhere. Cara noted there was nobody else standing at the bus stop.

Patrick Finney walked past the bus stop, smiled at the woman standing there and carried on walking. He waited a minute or so then doubled back and stopped at the side of the bus stop. He pretended to read the timetable and looked at his watch.

"Excuse me, Miss," he said to the woman. "I've left my watch at home. Do you have the time?"

She rummaged inside her handbag and took out a mobile phone.

"It's just gone seven."

"It's getting darker earlier, don't you think?" Finney commented.

She nodded but didn't reply.

"The moon is waning. It doesn't help. It doesn't help at all."

Cara Kenny watched what happened next without blinking. She watched as Finney raised something in the air and before the woman realised what was happening Finney moved in and the next moment the woman was on the ground. It was all over in seconds.

Finney looked up and down the street, took something out of his pocket and threw it down on top of the dead woman. He then crouched down and started to draw something on the pavement below the bus shelter. He glanced at the woman once more and set off down the road.

Cara knew she had to move quickly. She walked across the road to the bus stop and bent down over the woman. She was past saving. On her chest was a blue tie. Specks of blood had already soaked through the fabric and turned parts of the tie black. Cara took out a plastic bag and shoved the tie inside with the toe of her boot. She sealed it and set off in the direction Finney had gone.

* * *

O'Reilly didn't know about the press conference. He had no idea that Franklin Urban had made a complete fool out of himself in front of journalists from far and wide. He was also unaware of the gruesome discovery an old lady hoping to catch the Number 42 bus to St Peter Port was about to make at the bus stop in Vazon.

He cracked open another beer and looked out of the window at the building opposite the B&B. A woman was drying her hair by the window, totally oblivious to the events that were unfolding around her on the island. She was mouthing the words to a song O'Reilly couldn't hear but judging by the expression on her face it was an upbeat number.

The door to the room opened and O'Reilly jumped. He turned around and saw it was Cara. For the first time since O'Reilly had made her acquaintance, she had a smile on her face.

"You've found him, haven't you?" O'Reilly asked her.

"Even better," Cara said. "I have a plan. But I'm also here with some bad news."

"Bad news can wait. What's this plan?"

She took out a plastic bag and placed it on the table. She removed the tie. "Do you recognise this?"

"That's mine," O'Reilly said. "Where did you get it?"

"I didn't," Cara told him. "Finney did. He's killed again. I had to let it happen."

"You saw him kill someone?"

"It was the woman or you, Liam. He threw the tie on top of her when he was finished. He's trying to frame you."

"How the hell did he get my tie?"

"How do you think?"

It was all starting to make sense. O'Reilly remembered when Urban and his team searched his apartment there was no sign of the package Finney had sent, and the brick with the note attached was missing too. O'Reilly hadn't thrown them away and now Finney had left a tie belonging to O'Reilly at the scene of another murder.

"He's been inside my apartment," he said. "That bastard broke into my apartment. You mentioned something about a plan."

"I know where he's been staying," Cara said. "I'm going to play the same game as him, but we need to get out of here."

"Is this the bad news?"

"Your face is all over the place, Liam Cara said. "There was a press conference and every news site has posted your face out there. It's not safe here."

"Where are we going to go?"

"I was hoping you would be able to come up with an idea."

Something on the table caught O'Reilly's eye.

"I've got an idea," he said.

"Go on."

"Let's get out of here. I'll explain on the way."

CHAPTER THIRTY EIGHT

Detective Inspector Rob Crown was a troubled man. The Border Agency forensics officer's insides were churning after the debacle of the press conference. It was all wrong. In all his years in the Island Police he had never experienced such humiliation. He'd been forced to endure the embarrassment of an hour sitting next to DCI Franklin Urban and listening to the Head of the GBA talking himself further and further into a corner. The press was going to crucify him – that much was certain, but what was eating away at DI Crown wasn't Urban's incompetence, it was the treatment O'Reilly had received. Any teenager with an affinity for the Hardy Boys could see the Irish DI was being set up, but Urban's grudge against him had clouded his judgement to such an extent he would use anything he could to see O'Reilly put in his place.

It wasn't right and DI Crown needed to do something to reset the balance. His conscience and his professional courtesy demanded it. It was getting late but there was no time like the present. He picked up his phone and brought up the number. His finger hovered over the screen before he finally pressed, *call*.

DI Jim Peters answered immediately.

"Rob," he said. "It's a bit late for a social call, isn't it?"

"This isn't a social call, Jim," Rob said. "Can you talk?"

"Go on."

"I assume you heard about the press conference?"

"Who hasn't? Superintendent Hayes is on the phone to the CO as we speak. I have to say, your boss made a bit of a balls-up there."

"A bit?" Rob said. "I was sitting next to him the whole time. I wanted the floor to swallow me up. Anyway, that's not why I'm calling. Can we meet up at the lab?"

"What for?'

"Because I know for a fact O'Reilly had nothing to do with any of this and I think I might have come up with something that will prove it."

"I'm intrigued. You realise you're playing with fire here? Urban is going to have your balls for going up against him."

"I don't care, Jim," DI Crown said. "Between you and me I've got a feeling DCI Franklin Urban's days in the Island Police are numbered."

"You could be right."

"I am," DI Crown said.

"I'll be there in twenty minutes," DI Peters said.

* * *

"Where are we going?" Cara asked O'Reilly.

He'd packed his things and they'd left the B&B without letting the receptionist know he wouldn't be back.

"Church," O'Reilly told her. "It's a Protestant church so I hope you won't be offended. It's not far from here in La Planque."

"I gave up on religion when I was thirteen," Cara told him. "I just need to check something out first."

She turned left onto La Duannes and picked up the main road to Vazon.

"Where are we headed?" O'Reilly said.

"Patrick Finney is hiding out in a flat a mile or so from here," Cara said. "I want to show you so you'll know where to go when the time's right."

"I'm not following you."

"You'll know."

She slowed down and stopped outside a row of shops.

She pointed to a flat above the Newsagents. "The light is on. He's still there. Where is this church again?"

The string quartet were halfway through their first set when O'Reilly and Cara walked inside the Protestant Church. O'Reilly was surprised at how packed the place was. It was a mixed bunch inside – with young and old there to enjoy the unusual music. The quartet were playing an old 80s song and a few of the older crowd were dancing. A bar had been set up at the side of the church.

"This is different," Cara said.

"I knew you'd like it," O'Reilly said. "Can I buy you a drink?"

"I don't usually drink when I'm at work, but I think I'll make an exception tonight. Anything wet and alcoholic."

O'Reilly went to the bar and returned with two beers. The quartet had just launched into the opening bars of *Guns n' Roses' Sweet Child O' Mine.* The violinist was matching Slash's famous guitar intro note for note and from the expression on her face everyone could see she was enjoying every second of it.

Cara took the beer from O'Reilly and took a long swig. "Thanks. These guys are very good. How come an old detective like you ended up with tickets for something like this?"

"Fate," O'Reilly took a sip of his beer. "Somehow I ended up here – one of the blokes setting up sensed I was down and gave me two free tickets."

"The luck of the Irish?"

"You of all people should know that's all bull. There's no such thing as the luck of the Irish. It's a myth."

O'Reilly bought two more beers just in time. The string quartet were about to take a break and the rush to the bar in the interval was like a stampede of elephants. The lights were turned on and the sound of chattering voices was deafening.

"Let's get some air," Cara suggested. "It's stifling in here. I'm scared that someone recognises you too. It's too risky in here with the lights on."

They walked down the road towards the park. The gates were still open so O'Reilly headed for the bench he'd sat on earlier. The curious squirrel was nowhere to be seen.

"How did a nice young girl like you end up working for The Man?" O'Reilly asked.

"You don't end up working for The Man," Cara replied. "It's more complicated than that."

"I'm not going anywhere. I've got all the time in the world. How did you two meet?"

"Me and The Man go back a bit," Cara said. "Let's just leave it at that."

"Fair enough. How are you going to get Finney? I want to hear this plan of yours."

"You will. Is there someone you can trust? Someone on your team?"

"I always thought I could trust all of them," O'Reilly said. "But now I'm not so sure. Why do you ask?"

"Because you need someone on your side if this is going to work. Someone who won't ask too many questions."

"Katie Owen," O'Reilly said. "I can trust DC Owen."

"Grand. We'll start with her then."

CHAPTER THIRTY NINE

"What are we looking for?" DI Jim Peters asked.

He and DI Crown were sitting in the lab at the Island Police HQ.

"Something to rule O'Reilly out," DI Crown said. "Something we should have looked for a long time ago. Urban has been so hell bent on pinning everything on O'Reilly he hasn't even considered the fact that he's being set up. And that's exactly what this looks like to me."

"Why the sudden change of heart?"

"It's not sudden," DI Crown said. "It's been niggling away at all of us from the very start but Urban was adamant. What's the story with O'Reilly and the DCI anyway?"

"It was before you arrived here," DI Peters said. "O'Reilly had barely set foot on the island when a body was found washed up on the beach. The man's eyes had been poked out and his hands were amputated. If I remember correctly, he had a crude tattoo on his back. Then more bodies started to pile up and it was a real nasty one. It was O'Reilly's first investigation in charge, and he handled it brilliantly. Urban somehow got it in his head that the murders were drug related – the tattoos were the work of the Bulgarian mafia and as such it fell under the jurisdiction of the GBA. He muscled in on the case and kicked O'Reilly to the side."

"He seems to have a habit of doing that."

"Anyway," DI Peters continued. "O'Reilly maintained all along that the murders were nothing to do with drug lords and in the end, he was proved right. Urban was humiliated – O'Reilly made him look like an idiot and he hasn't forgotten about it. He will look for any opportunity to get even, and right now it looks like he's using this to get his revenge."

"He's willing to ruin a man's life just to get revenge?"

"Franklin Urban is a dangerous man," DI Peters said. "And not someone you clash heads with."

"He shouldn't be in this job."

"I've got a feeling he won't be for much longer. From what I heard from Anne's conversation with the CO, Urban's time on the island is slowly running out."

DI Crown brought up the photographs of the two chalk drawings. "I'm still waiting for confirmation from an expert, but I'm positive these were drawn by a left-handed person."

"You're right," Peters agreed. "You can see the artist started the drawing there." He pointed to the downward stroke on the woman's head. "If they were right handed, they would have started drawing on the opposite side."

"And O'Reilly isn't left-handed," DI Crown said. "But Patrick Finney is."

"This isn't enough to put O'Reilly in the clear," Peters argued. "Anyone could draw something like this with the other hand."

"I thought of that."

DI Crown tapped the pad and the Path report for Delores O'Connell appeared on the screen.

"Good Lord" DI Peters said after reading it. "The woman was barely alive to begin with. Her organs were busy shutting down one by one. She must have been in considerable pain. Whoever killed her actually put her out of her misery, but what does it prove?"

"I heard something. I forget where I heard it but there was a suggestion that Delores O'Connell could have been in on her own murder. It sounds ridiculous but what if this Patrick Finney monster offered her something in return for killing her? Some kind of compensation perhaps."

"He could have paid her family," Peters speculated. "It is possible. But there's no way to check."

"Let's look at this from another angle," DI Crown said. "Urban has concentrated all his efforts on the evidence that points to O'Reilly. He hasn't once considered anything that points away from him. We've got the TODs for both women – let's look at those. We know Delores O'Connell was killed between nine and nine-thirty on Monday because she was seen leaving the Snapper around nine and O'Reilly found her half an hour later. That's a tricky one because O'Reilly was covered in her blood and his fingerprints were found on the knife used to kill her. The other woman hasn't been identified yet, but she was killed sometime between nine and noon on Saturday. Where was O'Reilly between those times? Urban hasn't even bothered to check."

DI Peters thought hard. "Hold on, you say the woman found in the wheelie bin was killed sometime on Saturday morning?"

"That's right."

"O'Reilly was at work last weekend."

"Are you sure?"

"Pretty sure. We'd been working on these container thefts and I think everybody was on duty."

"It's easy enough to check."

"Why are you so keen to clear O'Reilly's name?" DI Peters asked. "What happened to the rivalry between the GBA and us lowly plebs?"

"I was under the impression we were all on the same side."

"Tell Franklin Urban that."

"And I detest injustice," DI Crown added. "DI O'Reilly has been treated like a common criminal and Urban hasn't even bothered to listen to his side of the story. He's maintained from the start that Patrick Finney is behind this and nobody has bothered to consider he might be right."

"We believed him, but our hands were bound when Urban stepped in and used everything to fuel his personal vendetta. I have to get going. I'll pass all this on to Superintendent Hayes."

"The Super and DCI Fish are getting married, aren't they?"

"In two weeks," DI Peters replied. "Between you and me the DCI reckons he'll be glad when the day comes to be honest. He's getting fed up of listening to wedding plans. He reckons he's glad he only has to do it once."

"I'll keep you in the loop if I find anything else."

"Thanks, Rob," Peters said. "I appreciate what you're doing."

CHAPTER FORTY

"What are we going to do?" O'Reilly asked Cara. "We can't sit out here all night."

"I need to wait until Finney leaves the flat," she told him. "He has to go out sometime."

"What exactly are you planning?"

"Do you know the most important rule when it comes to framing someone?"

"I've never actually given it much thought."

"The most crucial element is the fewer people who know the better. Stitching someone up is much easier if nobody else knows what you're up to. Someone is always willing to talk for the right price. Or the right amount of pain for that matter."

"It sounds like you're an expert on the subject."

"I told you, The Man and me go back a bit."

"What's he like?" O'Reilly asked. "Everybody has heard of him but nobody actually knows the man. What's he like?"

"It's difficult to explain," Cara sighed. "And not many people would understand."

"Try me," O'Reilly said. "I'm not going anywhere."

"When I was younger, I thought he was a monster. He did some horrible things but when you put it into perspective, he was no worse than a lot of other businessmen."

"He hurts people, Cara," O'Reilly said. "He's not a businessman – he's a criminal mastermind."

"He doesn't hurt people for fun. That's the difference between The Man and a lot of the scumbags back home. Some of those bastards are real psychopaths and sadists. There's always a reason for what he does."

"He still causes pain, Cara," O'Reilly said.

"And he happens to be helping you right now," she reminded him. "What about you? What's the story with you and Dad?"

"Dad?"

"I said The Man," Cara looked away. "You must have heard wrong."

O'Reilly knew for a fact he hadn't heard wrong. He knew exactly what he'd heard.

"So?" Cara urged. "What is it between you two? Why is someone like The Man willing to go to all this effort to help a former detective in the Gardai?"

"He doesn't like Paddy Finney very much."

Cara shook her head. "No, there's more to it than that. The Man doesn't like many people but he seems to have a soft spot for you. Why is that?"

"Must be my natural charm. What do we do now?"

"Can't we just stay and chat for a bit longer?" Cara asked. "I'm just getting to know you."

"There's not much to me," O'Reilly said. "I'm a sad Irish widower who ran away to this island to try and escape the past. That's about the size of it."

"The past isn't that easy to run away from, Liam. You can change your surroundings but you can't escape from what's inside your head."

"Wise words for one so young."

"What happened to your wife?" Cara asked.

"Cancer," O'Reilly said. "It's been a couple of years now. That's one of the reasons I came over here. Too many ghosts lurking in every corner."

"They're everywhere, you know. The ghosts I mean. We all have them."

"What about you, Cara," O'Reilly said. "You know everything about me – what's your story? I don't even know your full name."

"Kenny," she said. "My name is Cara Shannon Kenny. I'm twenty-nine and single and I also have a few ghosts but I'm not going to talk about them. It's getting cold. Let's find somewhere warmer."

They didn't speak as they drove. O'Reilly didn't know where they were going and he didn't ask. He thought back to what Cara had said in the park. He hadn't imagined it – she'd said *Dad* instead of The Man. Was Cara Kenny really the daughter of the most notorious criminal mind in Ireland? And if so, why had The Man sent his own flesh and blood over to the island to help him? It didn't make any sense. The Man knew Patrick Finney. He knew what Finney was capable of and yet he would risk his daughter's safety in order to help out a police detective.

The sea came into view in the distance and O'Reilly realised where they were. They were heading down La Grange towards the town centre.

"Where are we going?" he asked. "I live round the corner from here."

"You have to turn yourself in, Liam," Cara said in a grave voice.

"What the hell are you talking about?"

"It's the only way. You have to turn yourself in if this is going to work."

"What good will it do if I'm locked up?" O'Reilly couldn't believe what he was hearing. "How am I going to help you then?"

"You're not here to help me," Cara turned into the road where Police HQ was situated. "I'm here to help you, and you need to do as I say."

"No," O'Reilly said.

She ignored him and carried on driving. She turned right into the car park at the station and stopped next to the access door to the holding cells.

"Goodbye, Liam," she said.

"I'm not turning myself in," O'Reilly was adamant.

"It's the only way," Cara said. "You can do this in a dignified way or I can hold my hand on the hooter until someone comes out. Walk in there with your head held high and wait it out. It'll be alright."

"What are you going to do?"

"I'm going to beat Patrick Finney at his own game. And the less you know about that, the better. Goodbye, Liam."

O'Reilly found himself opening the car door and heading for the door to the station. He watched as The Man's daughter sped out of the car park and raced back up the street.

CHAPTER FORTY ONE

"Look at the drawing," DCI Tom Fish pointed to the crude chalk drawing on the ground in front of the dead woman.

"Number 7," DS Skinner read the number at the bottom. "Another one."

Fish and Skinner had been called out when an old woman had been found wandering the street babbling something about murder. A late-night jogger had calmed her down and managed to ascertain what had happened. The jogger phoned the Police as soon as he saw the body.

"Why isn't Urban involved?" DS Skinner asked. "If this is the same as the others, why isn't the GBA handling it?"

"You haven't seen the online news sites then?" Fish asked. "Urban made a bit of a tit out of himself in front of journalists from all over. I heard he's suspended."

"What did he do?"

"He told the whole world that O'Reilly was responsible for the recent murders."

"You're kidding?"

"It's no joke. And Urban was laughed at by the whole lot of them. I didn't realise how much respect people had for O'Reilly on this island. They passed the whole thing off as ludicrous, and they've printed as much on their forums and blogs."

"Do you think O'Reilly knows about it?" Skinner asked.

"I reckon he's keeping his head down until this blows over. Here's Peters."

The Head of Forensics had been as surprised as DS Skinner when he received the phone call. He'd just got back home after his meeting with DI Crown when Superintendent Hayes had phoned him.

"What have we got?" he asked DCI Fish and looked at the woman on the ground by the bus stop.

"We waited until you got here to see if she had any ID on her," Fish told him. "But there's another chalk drawing in the ground."
"Drawn by a left-handed man," Peters said.
"Excuse me?"
"Just thinking out loud. Henry is on his way, but I'll make a start while I'm waiting for him."

"This was Patrick Finney, wasn't it?" DS Skinner said to DCI Fish.
"Probably," Fish agreed. "He's getting out of control. And if he thinks he can pin this one on O'Reilly he's more insane than we thought."
"Are we going to investigate this with Finney as prime suspect?"
"He's the only suspect as far as I'm concerned. Franklin Urban's little game of revenge ended when that press conference ended, and I've got a feeling he's finished on this island and everywhere else in the police force too probably. He's made the Island Police look like imbeciles and we need to do something to rectify that."
"We need to catch Finney, you mean?"
"That's exactly what I mean, but I've got a feeling we're going to need O'Reilly's help to do that."

DI Peters walked over to them. "Her name is Patricia King. Her driving license was in her bag. She's had her throat cut, and she probably bled out within seconds. And if I were to hazard a guess, I'd say that the person who killed her was left-handed."
"What makes you say that?" DCI Fish asked.
"Most killers who kill this way slice the throat from behind the victim. It's much more effective than doing it from the front, and the wound on that poor woman's neck looks deeper on the left-hand side."
He demonstrated what he meant by running his left forefinger across his own neck.
"A leftie slices from right to left, and vice versa for a right-handed person."

An ambulance arrived at the same time as Superintendent Anne Haye's Range Rover appeared. She parked across the road from the bus stop.
"Looks like the wife is checking up on you, sir," DS Skinner said to DCI Fish.
Superintendent Hayes walked across the road to them.
"DI O'Reilly has turned up," she told them all.
"Where did they find him?" DS Skinner asked.
"They didn't – he came back on his own, about half an hour ago. Is there any indication he had any involvement in that?"
She pointed to the dead woman on the ground.
"Not yet," DI Peters replied. "You know he wasn't involved in any of them, don't you?"
"Of course I do," Superintendent Hayes said. "But Urban followed the evidence and the evidence alone. He didn't bother to stop and think why there was so much evidence against a fellow officer, and I believe he's going to pay dearly for that."
"What does the DI have to say for himself?" DS Skinner asked.
"I haven't spoken to him yet. PC London was manning the desk when he turned up – he hasn't been arrested and he told her he would wait in his office for further instructions."
"He's up to something," DCI Fish said.
"How can he be up to something cooped up in his office?" Superintendent Hayes said.
"You mark my words – that Irishman is up to something."

DS Henry Earle arrived and joined DI Peters next to the bus stop.
"What have we got?"
"Looks like Patrick Finney has struck again," The Head of Forensics told him. "There's another chalk drawing on the ground. O'Reilly has turned up."
"How's he doing?"

"How do you think he's doing? He's been treated like shit by the people who ought to have stood by him. He's probably feeling a bit pissed off by now. You know the drill. I'll leave you to it, and don't be surprised if you find something that links O'Reilly to the murder around here somewhere."

CHAPTER FORTY TWO

Cara Kenny had been waiting down the road from the Newsagents all night. The sun was coming up and the shop hadn't yet opened for the day. She ducked down further in the car seat when she saw the door to the side of the shop open. A man emerged and looked up and down the street. Patrick Finney pulled his collar up higher and made his way down the deserted road in the direction of the old church.

Cara waited ten minutes to make sure Finney didn't return and got out of the car. She walked across the street and examined the door Finney had recently come out of. It was locked but it was an old lock and it wouldn't pose too much of a problem. Cara glanced at the sign on the door of the Newsagents. There were twenty-five minutes before the shop opened.

After picking the lock Cara walked up the stairs to the room at the top. This door was going to be a bit trickier to open. It would be easy enough to kick in, but if Cara's plan was going to work that wasn't an option. It took her six minutes to finally break in and enter the room.

Inside was a bed, a single seater and a small chest of drawers with a kettle on top. Cara opened the top drawer and emptied the contents of the carrier bag she was carrying into it. The second drawer was empty but inside the bottom drawer, underneath a black sweater was a Smith and Wesson M&P SHIELD.

"Pansy," Cara said out loud. "You don't even carry a man's gun."

The small, lightweight pistol was popular at one stage amongst the wannabe gangsters in Dublin due to its ability to be easily concealed, but Cara preferred something more robust and obvious. The silencer looked home-made.

She picked it up and popped out the clip. She removed the six 9mm Luger bullets and reinserted the empty clip. There was another bullet in the chamber but she left that one alone.

She looked out of the window. The street was still deserted. Then she saw him. With his collar still rolled up he was walking back to the Newsagents.

Cara took out her phone and typed a simple message. Then she sat down on the bed to wait.

* * *

O'Reilly was dozing off in his office when the unfamiliar message tone sounded on his phone. He'd been inside his office since the previous night and he felt exhausted. He opened the phone and read the message and was out of the office in seconds.

PC London had just finished her shift on the front desk and was getting ready to leave.

"Kim," O'Reilly said. "I need everybody there is to get to this address over in Vazon."

He showed her the address Cara Kenny had sent him.

"Sir?" PC London said.

"Now, Kim," O'Reilly said. "Get hold of everybody you can and do as I say."

DC Owen walked in with DC Stone.

"Katie," O'Reilly said. "Andy, you're coming with me. Andy you're driving."

"What's going on, sir?" DC Stone asked. "I thought you'd done a runner. Assumpta is going spare."

"I'll fill you in on the way." O'Reilly turned to PC London. "I assume I'm free to go?"

"You always were, sir," the red-faced PC told him.

"Put your foot down, man," O'Reilly said to DC Stone. "I thought you knew how to drive."

"The traffic is bad, sir," the rat-faced DC said. "It's the morning rush hour."

"Step on it," O'Reilly said.

He was out of the car before Andy Stone brought it to a complete halt. "Wait here," he told DC Stone and DC Owen. "Wait five minutes then come up to the flat."

"But, sir," DC Owen said.

"Five minutes," O'Reilly repeated.

The Newsagents was opening its doors for the day as O'Reilly went through the side door and up the stairs to the flat. The door at the top was closed. O'Reilly stopped outside it and listened. Somebody was moving around inside. O'Reilly took a deep breath and opened the door wide.

Cara Kenny was on the bed. Her eyes were open and there was a small hole in the middle of her forehead.

"Stupid bitch thought she could catch me out, Smiley."

Patrick Finney had changed almost beyond recognition. The fifteen years behind bars had clearly taken their toll on him. His face was gaunt and pale and his once-charming eyes were bloodshot and haunted. He'd lost a lot of weight and his clothes were hanging off him.

"Cat got your tongue, Smiley."

Finney's voice was exactly how O'Reilly remembered it. The deep baritone was still the same.

"It's over, Finney," O'Reilly said. "You've killed for the last time."

Finney laughed and pointed the gun at O'Reilly. "You've come alone, I see. I knew you were stupid, but I'd forgotten how stupid you are."

O'Reilly looked at Cara Kenny's lifeless body on the bed. The Man's daughter was dead.

"You made a mistake," O'Reilly said to Finney. "Just like you did when you killed Ellie Finch."

"The pretty young DC?" Finney said and licked his lips. "I nearly deviated from the plan with lovely Ellie, but I managed to contain myself. It's your move, Smiley. You can take me in again, but you'll have to get past six of Luger's finest first."

"I hate guns," O'Reilly said and took a step closer.

"That's enough," Finney curled his finger around the trigger. "I'm walking out of here. You're going to watch me go."

"The Man isn't going to let this one go Paddy."

"I'm not afraid of The Man."

"You will be," O'Reilly took another step closer. "Especially when he finds out you killed his daughter."

This took a few seconds to sink in. Finney's eyes widened and the hand holding the gun started to shake.

"You're lying," he said.

"You'll soon find out. It's over, Paddy."

"Goodbye, Smiley."

The gun clicked as the firing pin met fresh air. Patrick Finney lowered it and looked at it like it was something he didn't recognise. He raised it again and another click was heard. The door burst open and four or five people stormed into the room.

CHAPTER FORTY THREE

"Interview with Patrick Duncan Finney commenced, 12:25," O'Reilly said. "Present Mr Finney, DI O'Reilly and DCI Fish. For the record, Mr Finney has waived his right to legal representation. It wouldn't do you any good anyway, would it, Paddy?"

"Get on with it, Smiley," Finney said and sat further back in his chair.

The handcuffs he was wearing did nothing to wipe the smug grin off his face, nor did the two uniformed officers standing sentry outside the door.

"I killed Miss Kenny," Finney's grin widened further still. "There you go. We're done. You got me."

"You killed Delores O'Connell, Judy Trevin and Patricia King," O'Reilly said. "There's no point in you denying it. You're going to be shipped back to Portlaoise and you'll spend the rest of your days there but there are still three murders that need clearing up and I hate that."

"You're barking up the wrong tree, Smiley."

"Paddy, you're not listening to me. Unsolved murders really piss me off, so I suggest you save us all a lot of time and energy and tell us about it."

"No comment," Finney said. "I bet you hate it when they say that too. Can I go now? If I leave now, I might get back before fish and chips. You really should try the fish and chips in Portlaoise."

"Tom," O'Reilly said to DCI Fish. "Do you want to do the honours?"

"It'll be my pleasure," the DCI replied and opened up a file in front of him. "Mr Finney do you recognise this?"

He passed him a photograph.

"It's my jumper," Finney replied. "What about it?"

"Can you explain how your jumper ended up with Delores O'Connell's blood on it?"

"What?"

"It's not important," DCI Fish told him. "What about this?"

This time it was a photograph of a brick and the note that was tied around the brick.

"Never seen them before," Finney said.

"They must have got into the drawer in the flat you were staying in by accident. And can you explain why there was a box containing thirty-thousand pounds in the flat? The box was addressed to Francis O'Connell. That wouldn't be any relation of Delores, would it?"

O'Reilly spotted a crack in Finney's defiant demeanour. It was a faint crack but it was one he was going to chip away at.

"We also found a tie in the chest of drawers," he said. "The blood on the tie was a match to Patricia King. How do you explain that?"

"The tie..." Finney stopped there.

"Go on," O'Reilly urged. "You were about to tell us about the tie. You were about to tell us how you broke into my house, and stole the tie together with the brick and the box with what I assume was fibres from Judy Trevin's mohair jumper. That's right, isn't it?"

"You're not getting anything else out of me, Smiley."

"I don't need anything else. You were caught on CCTV at my apartment complex."

This was a blatant lie but O'Reilly didn't care.

"There weren't any cameras," Finney said.

"So, you admit you were there?"

"No comment."

"We forgot to show him the other photograph," DCI Fish said.

"Silly me," O'Reilly said. "I forgot all about that one."

"What photograph?" Finney said.

O'Reilly slid the last photo across the table. "This one. Names and dates and numbers, all written in chalk. It was pretty stupid of you to draw these on the side of the bed."

Finney looked at the photo and the colour in his face started to drain away. "What the hell is this? I didn't do this?"

"It was there in your room, Paddy," O'Reilly said. "Together with the money for Mrs O'Connell's son, the brick thrown through my window, the tie with the blood on it and.." He looked at DCI Fish. "Have I left anything out?"

"I don't think so," Fish said.

Finney glared at O'Reilly. The smug grin had vanished and he seemed smaller somehow.

"How? You set me up. You set me up you fecking bastard."

"Now now, Paddy," O'Reilly said. "That's a serious allegation to throw at a respectable detective inspector."

"You fecking bastard," Finney said again. "You set me up."

"It's a horrible feeling, isn't it? I think we'll finish up there, Tom. Mr Finney isn't looking too well. Interview with Patrick Finney ended 12:40."

CHAPTER FORTY FOUR

"Are you alright, Dad?" Assumpta asked.

"Grand," O'Reilly replied. "Just grand. Victoria and me are off to Tenerife next week and I can't wait. It'll do me the world of good to get away from the island for a while."

Things hadn't been quite the same since O'Reilly returned to work. His colleagues looked at him differently somehow. O'Reilly wasn't sure if they were acting out of sympathy for what he'd been through or because they felt some semblance of guilt. Even though every one of them had believed him there was a sense that perhaps they should have done more to help. O'Reilly had made it clear that there was nothing any of them could have done. All of their hands had been tied when Franklin Urban took over, but still their collective consciences felt a pang of regret for not sticking their necks out more.

The GBA had a new face at the helm. DCI Franklin Urban had been given a choice: either he take an early retirement package or face instant dismissal and of course he opted for the former. Nobody had seen him since his fiasco of a press conference and the CO had made it a prerequisite for his early retirement that he issue a press release stating it was his decision and his decision alone to pursue O'Reilly the way he did. He put it down to stress due to overwork and stated that was the reason for his early retirement.

Patrick Finney lasted another six days in Portlaoise Prison. One of the guards found him in his cell covered in blood. He'd received sixty-two stab wounds to his face and body and the guard only knew it was Finney from the name on his prison scrubs. Nobody admitted to the murder, but everybody knew who was responsible. Cara Kenny's death had been avenged.

Bram bashed into the cat flap and darted outside. The flap swung a few times then stopped.

"He's going to break that thing if he's not careful," O'Reilly said. "Do you want some coffee?"

"I've not long had one."

O'Reilly's phone started to ring. He picked it up and looked at the screen. The number had been withheld. His heart started to beat faster. He'd been expecting the call but still he could feel the throbbing of his heart in his chest. He took the phone to the living room.

"O'Reilly," he answered it.

"It's done.'

"It is," O'Reilly said.

The Man stayed silent.

"I'm really sorry about Cara," O'Reilly said. "She was a remarkable woman."

"She was her mother, through and through."

It had taken O'Reilly a while to figure out why Cara had done what she'd done. She'd broken into Finney's flat, knowing full well he knew what she was doing. She'd waited for him to return and sent O'Reilly the message. She told him what she'd planted inside the room, and she told him to come now. The bit O'Reilly found hardest to fathom out was why she'd left the bullet in the chamber. Then it occurred to him that it was all part of her plan. She needed O'Reilly to catch him red-handed with a dead body. She'd sacrificed herself to do that and O'Reilly would never forget her.

"I believe Paddy Finney is a dead man," O'Reilly said.

"Finney was a dead man the second he pulled that trigger," The Man said. "Our business is done."

"Thank you," O'Reilly said. "I can never repay you for this."

"You know your debt to me increased a thousand-fold when Cara's heart stopped beating, Smiley?"

"I understand," O'Reilly said without even thinking.

"Just so we're clear."

"Clear as the Liffey in February," O'Reilly said.

He took a deep breath to compose himself.

"Clear as the Liffey in February," he said once more but the line had already gone dead.

THE END

Printed in Great Britain
by Amazon

71538693R00119